THE
TRUTH
ABOUT
TEACHING

Sara Miller McCune founded SAGE Publishing in 1965 to support the dissemination of usable knowledge and educate a global community. SAGE publishes more than 1000 journals and over 800 new books each year, spanning a wide range of subject areas. Our growing selection of library products includes archives, data, case studies and video. SAGE remains majority owned by our founder and after her lifetime will become owned by a charitable trust that secures the company's continued independence.

Los Angeles | London | New Delhi | Singapore | Washington DC | Melbourne

THE TRUTH ABOUT TEACHING

AN EVIDENCE-INFORMED GUIDE FOR NEW TEACHERS

GREG ASHMAN

Los Angeles | London | New Delhi
Singapore | Washington DC | Melbourne

Los Angeles | London | New Delhi
Singapore | Washington DC | Melbourne

SAGE Publications Ltd
1 Oliver's Yard
55 City Road
London EC1Y 1SP

SAGE Publications Inc.
2455 Teller Road
Thousand Oaks, California 91320

SAGE Publications India Pvt Ltd
B 1/I 1 Mohan Cooperative Industrial Area
Mathura Road
New Delhi 110 044

SAGE Publications Asia-Pacific Pte Ltd
3 Church Street
#10-04 Samsung Hub
Singapore 049483

Editor: James Clark
Editorial assistant: Diana Alves
Production editor: Martin Fox
Copyeditor: Elaine Leek
Proofreader: Audrey Scriven
Indexer: Silvia Benvenuto
Marketing manager: Dilhara Attygalle
Cover design: Sheila Tong
Typeset by: C&M Digitals (P) Ltd, Chennai, India
Printed in the UK

Library of Congress Control Number: 2018931189

British Library Cataloguing in Publication data

A catalogue record for this book is available from the
British Library

ISBN 978-1-5264-2086-2
ISBN 978-1-5264-2087-9 (pbk)

At SAGE we take sustainability seriously. Most of our products are printed in the UK using responsibly sourced
papers and boards. When we print overseas we ensure sustainable papers are used as measured by the PREPS
grading system. We undertake an annual audit to monitor our sustainability.

Dedication

For Jo, Rose and Catherine

CONTENTS

ABOUT THE AUTHOR

 Greg Ashman grew up in the UK. In 1997, after studying Natural Sciences at Cambridge, he began training as a teacher at the Institute of Education in London. He went on to teach in three London comprehensive schools and took on roles including head of science, assistant headteacher and deputy headteacher. In 2010 he moved to Ballarat, Australia, with his young family. Since then, he has worked as Head of Mathematics at Ballarat Clarendon College. During this time he has developed an interest in education research and is currently undertaking a PhD in Instructional Design, as well as taking on the role of Head of Research at Clarendon.

PREFACE

Despite the vast volume of education research available, teaching cannot claim to be an evidence-based profession. More strikingly, perhaps, teaching could not be truly evidence-based, even if we committed to that goal as a profession. This speaks to the quality of education research but also to the fact that teachers juggle different priorities, and attitudes to education are as much philosophical as they are technical.

Instead, we can hope to be evidence-*informed*. We can note the evidence where it exists and the holes where it does not, and we can make decisions against this background. Adopt this mindset and there is a vast literature out there that can inform what we do in practical and meaningful ways.

In this book I aim to present the most vital evidence that a new teacher needs to know about and, where the evidence is lacking or inconclusive, weave it together with craft knowledge to make something that you can wear as you enter the classroom for the first time. I want you to be prepared so that you can avoid common and obvious mistakes.

Teaching is strangely ahistorical. Huge events are forgotten. Large-scale experiments are ignored, doomed to be repeated by later generations who appear not to realise what has gone before. Perhaps this is because we are always looking to the future, as we help craft the minds of the generation to come.

In this book we will therefore start with a little historical context. It is impossible to convey the entire history of education in a single chapter, but I wish to provide just enough so that you can identify common themes and interpret the evidence I later present in this context.

We will then explore the issue of classroom management. It is vital for new teachers to get this right. Most new teachers are aware of this and it is the issue that keeps them awake at night. Yet, I don't think

I was adequately prepared when I first started teaching and this seems to be a common experience among teachers I know in real life and through social media. There are reasons why classroom management is downplayed, and it is important to know what these are.

We will then introduce the science of learning. Cognitive science has made great strides over the last few decades, and yet it is only in the last few years that it is starting to inform classroom practice. Some of the findings are counterintuitive and others may feel like common sense. How do we know when to follow our instincts? We look to experimental evidence.

Next, we will explore explicit forms of teaching and the alternatives. There are good reasons to apply both approaches at certain times and for particular aims, and we will attempt to clearly map this territory before rolling up our sleeves and delving into the practical aspects of planning lessons and assessing student learning.

Classroom technology is a major issue that has a higher profile than is perhaps justified. This attention is no doubt driven by the fact that there are products to sell. We will examine good uses of technology and how to spot a white elephant.

The teaching of reading is the most examined area in all of education, and so we will look at this issue and the reasons why the use of phonics – relating letters to their corresponding sounds – has become so controversial. This chapter is not just for teachers of early reading, it is illustrative of the role of evidence in the wider education debate.

Finally, we will ask what it is to be a teacher? Why do we choose this profession, why do teachers quit and how can you keep going when times are tough?

I want you to keep teaching. I want you to enjoy the rewards that I have enjoyed. Teaching is not just something you do and, in order to be successful, you will have to live it. Knowledge of the great debates will help you gain perspective and may spark your curiosity. After all, a job is easier to do if you find it interesting. And knowledge of the evidence will allow you to spot bad ideas and avoid the embrace of snake-oil salesmen, of whom there are far too many.

But let's not focus on the negative. A knowledge of the evidence helps us in our goal to do a wonderful thing: to pass on our civilisation to the next generation; to enable everyone to live rich and fulfilling lives. As a teacher, you conjure understanding where there was none. You are a magician.

That's pretty special.

ACKNOWLEDGEMENTS

My wonderful wife, Jo, has been critical in enabling this book to be written. It also would not exist without the support of the online education community, and especially Andrew Smith, who encouraged my early blogging.

I have been influenced by many educators throughout my career, including Jenny Frost, Robin Turner, Mark Bulldeath, Peter Woods, Marion and Mike Hardy, Narinder Birdi, Arwel Jones, Terry Farrell, Sue Gould and many more. I am particularly grateful to Jan McClure and David Shepherd, who welcomed me into a school where research is held in high regard, sparking my interest and offering unwavering support as I pursued this interest.

Finally, I must thank all of those who have read drafts of the manuscript. My PhD supervisors, John Sweller and Slava Kalyuga, have offered thoughts on the science of learning and Kevin Wheldall provided some challenging feedback on classroom management. James Clark at Sage has gently advised me throughout the writing process and the book is far better for his input. Any mistakes that remain are my own responsibility.

1

A SHORT HISTORY OF EDUCATION

Key Points

This chapter will:

- Outline some important developments in the history of education that affect teaching today
- Describe the philosophy of educational progressivism and attempt to explain its origins
- Look at how progressivism has waxed and waned in response to important events
- Ask how different education systems have been shaped by educational philosophies
- Show that investing more in education does not necessarily lead to gains in learning
- Suggest that we need to focus resources on initiatives that have a positive impact

A natural progression

As the new century advanced, key thinkers became increasingly concerned that school-based education was not adequately preparing young people for the demands of an unpredictable future. Some claimed that in the 20th century education would become ever-more important and take on a previously unknown 'burden of responsibility', but that this would require teachers to make use of new methods, materials and types of experiences (Bobbitt, 1918). One of the methods that showed promise was project-based learning.

William Heard Kilpatrick made the case for project-based learning in his 1918 essay 'The Project Method' (Kilpatrick, 1918). To Kilpatrick, involvement in a project was a 'purposeful act'. A girl engaged in dressmaking, for instance, is pursuing a project that has meaning, is motivating and has a clear objective. Similarly, a boy or a group of children who create a school newspaper will have a clear goal. The value of projects was that children would invest their 'whole heart' into them rather than acting through compulsion.

This stress on the motivational aspect of project work is in keeping with Kilpatrick's role as a leading light of America's Progressive Education Association. A key element of early 20th century progressive education philosophy was that learning should be natural – even joyful – and so must follow the contours of children's natural interests and be based in the activities they are naturally inclined to participate in (Egan, 2002). This implies a hands-off approach, where students figure things out for themselves with the teacher offering only guidance.

These ideas closely follow John Dewey who, in 1913, called time on the argument between those who wanted to make subjects interesting for students and those who preferred to emphasise the role of student effort. Instead, Dewey suggested that if we recognise there are 'certain powers within the child' that urgently need developing then, by following these natural, developmental impulses, students will be absorbed and whole-hearted, and learning will never be drudgery (Dewey, 1913). Dewey painted a picture of a unicorn that generations of teachers have been hunting.

As John Dewey later explained, while discussing the relative merits of different educational approaches, 'There is … no point in the philosophy of progressive education which is sounder than its emphasis upon the importance of the participation of the learner in the formation of the purposes which direct his activities in the learning process' (Dewey, 1938).

If any of this feels familiar, then that is because the philosophy of a natural form of learning, that follows the contours of children's interests, is still a powerful force in contemporary education, as well as being one that accurately attracts the 'progressive' label. And it is important that we pay progressive education its due, follow Dewey's example and describe it as a 'philosophy' rather than think of it as a bag of teaching tricks. Progressive education starts from principles and then selects curricula, teaching methods and even the objectives of education accordingly. Progressive education is ultimately about what educators *believe* education *is* rather than any classroom task.

Progressive education is not progressive politics. Instead, it represents a philosophy of learning that can be adopted regardless of political views. Although currently a default position of many on the political left, perhaps due to its name, progressive education was once the philosophy of Giovanni Gentile, Mussolini's education minister. As such, it drew criticism from the Marxist philosopher Antonio Gramsci (Mayo, 2014). Progressivism tends to emphasise the individual, something that is often more a concern of the political right. And it is important to note that a belief that education is about the unfolding of a natural plan does not compel us to believe that everyone has the same natural plan. Some students may be naturally fitted for leadership and others for factory work. This is the implication of any argument in favour of nurturing individual talents (e.g. Robinson, 2017).

There are many teachers who, if asked, would claim no educational philosophy. They would insist that they are pragmatists who draw upon different methods and tactics as required. But this is not true. Everyone has a set of beliefs about teaching, even if they lie largely hidden. You either believe that education should be a natural process, like the unfolding of a flower, or you do not. You cannot believe this for some of the time or for part of a lesson. Perhaps you disagree with Dewey and believe that some objectives of education are worth having but require an element of drudgery to get there, and that they therefore need to be set and monitored by the teacher? If so, that's part of your philosophy.

These are the two main ways of thinking about education. It is either a natural, drawing-out of something from within, or it is an effortful, sometimes painful process of passing knowledge from one generation to the next; a process that is not particularly natural. The dispute between these two positions has echoed through the ages.

Empty vessels

Educators have long taken inspiration from Ancient Greece. In the writings of Plato, we have an early description of the ideal curriculum for philosophers and leaders, provided by a form of boarding school for which students would be selected by aptitude at an early age. These ideas influenced later educational thinkers such as Jean-Jacques Rousseau (Jackson, 2012).

Plato believed that truths were immutable, and that education was the process of drawing out truths that people once knew in a previous life but have forgotten due to the corrupting influence of the world. He disliked the format of an audience listening to a poet reciting Homer, because he thought this was too passive, with no room for challenge or discussion. Instead, he provided his own instructional model by writing down the dialogues of his teacher, Socrates. Socrates constantly questioned the assumptions of those he conversed with (Jackson, 2012). This style has become known as 'Socratic questioning' and has gained popularity as a teaching approach (see Paul and Elder, 2007 for an overview).

Plutarch, a first century Greek essayist, is also an influence on education today, if for no other reason than an often-misattributed quote that 'the mind does not require filling like a bottle, but rather, like wood, it only requires kindling to create in it an impulse to think independently and an ardent desire for the truth' (Babbitt, 1927). Versions of this saying have been attributed to Socrates as well as W.B. Yeats (O'Toole, 2013). For instance, Gert Biesta deployed the Yeats version at the opening of his influential book *The Beautiful Risk of Education* (Biesta, 2015). Plutarch's analogy is most often used to implicitly or explicitly support a theory of learning known as 'constructivism' (e.g. Kuhs and Flake, 1993).

The philosophy of constructivism asserts that people do not simply receive ideas from others. Instead, they must construct meaning for themselves, or perhaps as part of a group effort. Many educators then take the additional, if not inevitable (Mayer, 2004), step of drawing implications for methods of teaching; that we should avoid trying to transmit ideas through lecturing and instead focus on methods that allow students to figure things out and make connections for themselves (see Perkins, 1999). In this sense, constructivism follows, and perhaps derives from, early 20th century progressivism.

Plutarch is an odd recruit to this cause. His famous quote comes from an essay about listening to lectures. It was written for Nicander, a young man who had finished formal schooling, and it consists of advice on how to continue with his education. Plutarch is concerned that young people are more interested in gossip or a 'wordy brawl' than they are in listening to serious advice about their duties. The quote is thus advice for the one who *listens* to a lecture rather than the one who delivers it. Plutarch is arguing for active listening rather than for simply basking in the glow of someone else's fine rhetoric. To some extent, this is supportive of constructivism.

However, Plutarch is generally in favour of listening and it seems unlikely that he would condemn the practice of lecturing. At another point in the essay, he concludes that, 'As skilful horse-trainers give us horses with a good mouth for the bit, so too skilful educators give us children with a good ear for speech, by teaching them to hear much and speak little' (Babbitt, 1927). This quote is less well known.

If we wish to understand Plutarch's attitude to formal education, an issue more relevant to the purpose of this book, then we should perhaps turn to a different essay, *The Education of Children*, although we should bear in mind that Plutarch's authorship is disputed. This essay sets out the case for education being built upon three components: nature, reason and habit. In other words, children have some natural capacities that can be improved by explicit training and then mastered through practice. As Plutarch, or the unknown author, states, 'Indifference ruins a good natural endowment, but instruction amends a poor one; easy things escape the careless, but difficult things are conquered by careful application'. This seems a surprisingly modern understanding of the process of learning.

On the other hand, lacking our present knowledge of genetics and heredity, the essay associates a superior nature with nobility of birth, cautioning men against cohabiting with courtesans and concubines. There is even advice against having sex when drunk, for fear of producing offspring with a love of the booze.

Master of puppets

The modern concepts of progressive education and constructivism draw heavily on the work of Jean-Jacques Rousseau (Rosenow, 1980;

Krahenbuhl, 2016), an 18th century Enlightenment philosopher who in many ways anticipated the Romantic movement.

Rousseau's great work on education is *Emile*, a novel about the tutoring of the eponymous hero. Rousseau's aim is to show how a perfect citizen may be moulded and, frankly, it's a little creepy. Emile's tutor, Jean-Jacques, joins him as a baby and is with him day and night, shaping his thoughts and experiences. The objective is to convince Emile that he has total freedom, that he never has to do anything he doesn't seek to do. Yet, Emile is not free because he is constantly being psychologically manipulated in his choices, with the aim of producing the perfect citizen.

Rousseau gave inspiration to the later progressive movement with its aim of marrying the processes of education to a child's natural inclinations. However, it is debatable whether Rousseau's intentions have been fully understood (Rosenow, 1980). It is still an open question as to how we can follow a child's natural impulses and yet also shape them to a desired end.

In the years following Rousseau's death, the nature of childhood underwent a significant change in the popular imagination, or at least the imagination of the middle and upper classes. In literature, the rational and flawed child of the 19th century gave way to the innocent and perfect child, under the growing influence of the romantic movement (MacLeod, 1992; Austin, 2003). Once the view takes hold that children do not need correction, that they have an essentially benign nature that is corrupted only by adults, a hands-off form of education will widen and deepen in appeal.

Sputnik shock

By the 1950s, the philosophy of progressive education was dominant in the United States' public-school system and teacher education colleges, and this was starting to generate something of a backlash. One key area of concern was reading. Progressives tended to favour methods of teaching reading that focused on whole words, or even sentences, rather than breaking words up into their components and relating these to the sound of the word. This trend provoked Rudolf Flesch to write his 1955 classic, *Why Johnny Can't Read And What You Can Do About It* (Flesch, 1955). The teaching of reading is central to the story of education and we will return to it in Chapter 10.

Although it was the dominant philosophy, it is impossible to know how many teachers fully subscribed to progressivism and applied its methods. Elements of older teaching styles probably survived in many schools. Which is why the impact of progressivism on the curriculum is arguably more significant than its impact on the act of teaching itself. Indeed, E.D. Hirsch has argued convincingly that a progressive-inspired curriculum reform led to a decline in the educational performance of students in France (Hirsch, 2016).

At best, progressivism is ambivalent about traditional subjects. At worst, it is openly hostile, seeking to replace them with studies that are more closely aligned to the child and his or her immediate surroundings and interests. By the 1950s, these centred on generic 'life adjustment' goals, similar to the goals we might now term 'soft skills'. As Dewey explains, 'Not knowledge or information, but self-realization, is the goal. To possess all the world of knowledge and lose one's own self is as awful a fate in education as in religion. Moreover, subject-matter never can be got into the child from without' (Dewey, 1902).

An illustrative example of the attitude to traditional subjects is the way that history was largely replaced in America by the 'expanding horizons' model of social studies. Instead of young children learning about the Romans, a people too distant from their own experience to comprehend, they would be asked to find out about their family tree or explore their local environment, gradually working outwards until, at some stage they may never reach, they are developmentally ready to tackle other times and peoples. It is as if children cannot imagine themselves into other places. As Kieran Egan suggests, this does not seem tenable when you consider the love they have for fairy stories and tales about talking animals (Egan, 1980).

It is therefore understandable that the inevitable backlash against progressive education would include criticism of the effect on the curriculum.

Writing in 1950, Mortimer Smith took on the curriculum issue. Smith described himself as a layperson, having not worked in education but instead having been a volunteer on a school board. He took the time to digest and explain his understanding of educational philosophy in general, and John Dewey in particular.

Smith's book, *And Madly Teach*, devoted a section to criticising the progressive 'doctrine' that 'the curriculum must be based upon the child's needs, interests and abilities'. He gives the example of a child who is passionate about history but whom maths fills with 'ennui', and he asks whether we should really follow these interests or whether we should persist with teaching maths in the service of a broad and balanced education. Smith is sceptical when confronted with utopian visions of how a young farm-hand would learn through compelling practical experience on an idyllic farm, pointing out that many such farm-hands move to the city, if given the choice, and that most children do not enjoy work of any kind (Smith, 1950).

The 1950s saw the publication of similar tomes with similar aims to that of Smith. The historian and professor Arthur Bestor released *Educational Wastelands* (Bestor, 1953), and former professor Albert Lynd released *Quackery in the Public Schools* (Lynd, 1953). A reviewer in the *New York Times* found much to agree with Lynd about, particularly on the watering down of the curriculum, but he did not care for the title and Lynd's general impatience, an impatience worth reflecting on from our 21st century perspective (Duffus, 1953).

The temperature was therefore rising without quite coming to the boil. It took a 58-centimetre polished metal sphere to do that: Sputnik 1. The fact that, in 1957, the Soviet Union had been able to place the first satellite in Earth orbit seemed to highlight a worrying gap in science and technological advancement between the two superpowers.

In March 1958, *Life* magazine ran an article on the 'crisis in education'. Beginning with the words, 'For years, most critics of U.S. education have suffered the curse of Cassandra – always to tell the truth, seldom to be listened to or believed', before profiling two young men, one American and the other Russian. The Russian student is serious about studying and tackles challenging technical content with the goal of becoming a physicist, whereas the American student is likeable and doesn't take school too seriously. The Russian has read Shakespeare, but the American has only managed to read *Kidnapped*, by Robert Louis Stevenson. In America, 'A quarter century has been wasted with the squabbling over whether to make a child well-adjusted or teach him something' (*Life*, 1958).

The reaction to Sputnik saw the federal government intervene in education in a manner it usually avoided, sponsoring the production of curriculum materials and bringing academics and teachers together with the aim of the public-school system better serving the needs of higher education. However, as the years progressed, the panic faded. America developed its own space technologies, culminating in beating the Soviet Union in the race to place people on the Moon. Over time, educational initiatives associated with the Sputnik crisis lost federal funding, fizzled out or became absorbed into the wider milieu (Rutherford, 1997) such that the intellectual and bureaucratic centres of American education largely returned to the pre-1957 consensus.

American education is periodically convulsed by panics like the Sputnik crisis, with similar arguments rehearsed and an eventual equilibrium restored. Another example is the response to 'A Nation at Risk', a 1983 report about lax standards of academic work and behaviour that was written in stirring language that captured America's attention (Ravitch, 2000). Arguably, the current focus on Science, Technology, Engineering and Maths (STEM) subjects is a panic in a similar vein.

Satellites

Ideas that took root in America would go on to influence education in Britain, Australia and eventually the whole world. However, each system had its own peculiarities and preoccupations.

The publication of the Plowden Report was a seminal moment in the UK. It was the work of the Central Advisory Council for Education (England) and was commissioned in 1963. Following several years of work that included visiting many classrooms, the council's report was finally published in 1967 and titled *Children and their Primary Schools*. Nevertheless, it is more popularly known as 'The Plowden Report,' after the influential chair of the council, Lady Bridget Plowden.

Many items addressed by Plowden are issues that would now represent a consensus position in education, such as a call for a ban on physical punishment, and demonstrate the forward-thinking nature of the Council. Other items addressed issues involving administration and management of schools. However, the report did not stop here. It also delved into the realm of teaching methods, arguing for a more child-centred, progressive approach.

This becomes clearest in Chapter 16 of Plowden, the chapter that describes the authors' understanding of learning. Play is heavily emphasised as desirable and as an activity that leads to learning. Teachers should see themselves as facilitators. The report's authors are concerned that previous advocates for experience-based education have downplayed the value of knowledge. Instead, 'activity and experience, both physical and mental, are often the best means of gaining knowledge and acquiring facts'. Students should also be given plenty of choice. This is clear from passages in the report that sketch out approving vignettes. It is also made explicit. For instance:

> Skills of reading and writing or the techniques used in art and craft can best be taught when the need for them is evident to children. A child who has no immediate incentive for learning to read is unlikely to succeed because of warnings about the disadvantages of illiteracy in adult life. There is, therefore, good reason for allowing young children to choose within a carefully prepared environment in which choices and interest are supported by their teachers, who will have in mind the potentialities for further learning. (Central Advisory Council for Education, 1967)

As ever, it is difficult to tell exactly what effect these recommendations had on ordinary classrooms and whether teachers changed their approaches in response. However, by the time of the 1975 ORACLE project, a study of teacher behaviours in English primary schools, it was possible to start making some inferences. Teachers appeared to require students to complete a lot of individual work, some of dubious value, and teacher-student interactions were often at the individual level. There was little whole-class teaching and yet there was also little of the group work encouraged by Plowden (Galton, 1987).

Australian education continues to be informed by a progressive philosophy, particularly in the area of curriculum design. A notable initiative of the 1990s and early 2000s was, 'Outcomes Based Education' (OBE), which took an interesting philosophical stance. The idea was that curriculum cannot be designed until the ultimate outcomes of education have been established. It was not the job of teachers to deliver a specific curriculum but rather to design a curriculum to support these outcomes. OBE was highly individualised, with standardised tests being downplayed in favour of students being given as many attempts as they need to demonstrate an outcome. Moreover, priority was placed on students enjoying the process of learning, which was seen as more important than the content being learnt.

In OBE, we can see some key progressive principles, such as individualisation, enjoyment and a downplaying of traditional curriculum subjects. However, these are mixed with novelties arising from antipathy towards standardised testing, such as the idea of defining many outcomes and identifying them on a continuum. If this sounds bureaucratic, it was. OBE was presented idealistically rather than practically. The main complaint of teachers seems to have been about the lack of guidance on implementation and the vague nature of the outcomes, particularly given that each school was intended to write its own curriculum, rather than a critique of the ideas behind OBE (McNaught and Berlach, 2007). In this sense, the current bureaucratic problems associated with Scotland's 'Curriculum for Excellence' seem to echo those of OBE (Ashman, 2017).

More recently, Australia's national curriculum has drawn heavily on progressive philosophy. While maintaining some traditional subject areas, and specifying the use of phonics over whole-word methods of reading, it has added lots of generic 'life adjustment' goals such as 'personal and social capability' and, for primary age children, it has collapsed humanities subjects together into an expanding horizons social studies curriculum reminiscent of 1940s America. Even within traditional subjects such as science, academic content is downplayed, and experience-based objectives are emphasised, such as 'With guidance, plan and conduct scientific investigations to find answers to questions' (Australian Curriculum, 2018).

In addition to curriculum design, Australian education academics have tended to favour more progressive, experiential teaching methods. One popular approach is known as 'productive pedagogies'. Based upon ideas originally developed in the United States, productive pedagogies is an attempt to define quality teaching, research its prevalence in schools and train teachers to use these strategies.

Rooted in constructivism, productive pedagogies draws a distinction between 'lower-order thinking' and 'higher-order thinking'. Teachers should aim to induce higher-order thinking in their students by asking them to manipulate or synthesise ideas in order to create new meanings, solving problems and discovering new understandings in the process. Lower-order thinking is characterised by students being asked to receive factual information (pre-specified knowledge) or to complete processes using specific routines and algorithms (Lingard et al., 2001; Gore et al., 2017). The caution against algorithms is a common one in the field of mathematics education where some commentators draw on constructivism to argue that students should figure out problems for themselves rather than apply standard procedures such as column addition or long division (e.g. Kamii and Dominick, 1998).

Things can only get better

I began training as a teacher in London in October 1997, five months after Tony Blair first won office as Britain's Prime Minister. One of Blair's election slogans was 'Education, Education, Education', and he certainly made it a priority. From 1997 until Blair's Labour Party finally lost office in 2010, education spending grew dramatically. From the 1999–2000 financial year to the 2009–2010 financial year, education spending increased by 5.1% per year, once inflation is taken into account (Chowdry and Sibieta, 2011).

The headline attainment figure that was usually quoted by English newspapers over this time was the percentage of students gaining five or more A* to C grades in GCSE examinations, a set of elective exams taken at age 16. According to this figure, attainment rose dramatically in England from 1997 to 2010, giving encouragement that standards had risen. However, a separate analysis based upon English students' performance in various international assessments shows a fairly stable level of achievement across this period (Coe, 2013). What actually happened? Which measure is right?

The obvious explanation is to pay more heed to the international results and suspect that GCSE grades became subject to grade inflation. England's GCSE examinations were not cohort-referenced during this time. Cohort-referencing is the practice of always awarding the same proportion of each grade. For example, you might always give 5% of students an A* grade, regardless of the quality of work. Clearly, if grades had been cohort-referenced then we could not have seen a rise in the headline figures. Instead, they were intended to be criterion-referenced, with criteria describing the quality of work required for each grade. Yet it is hard to see how we can decide that an assessment criterion in, say, graphic design represents the equivalent academic standard of a criterion in physics. Without anything to nail these exam grades to the wall, it became possible for exams to gradually become easier and for grade boundaries to drift downwards. Add to this the fact that different exams were created by exam boards who competed for custom, and that schools were incentivised by account-ability measures to gain the best possible results, and we can see the systemic motivation for why this might occur, even if nobody ever made a conscious and explicit decision to dumb down the exams.

On reflection, the finding that standards did not improve seems extraordinary given the increase in expenditure. Why didn't we get what we had paid for? The answer seems to be that the extra money was not spent wisely.

Some early initiatives of the Blair government, such as the National Numeracy Strategy, were clearly based upon the best available evidence (Reynolds and Muijs, 1999). However, as time passed, it became clear to me, as a teacher working in the system, that two factors were driving much of the reform: a bureaucratic approach that saw good ideas such as formative assessment (Black andWiliam, 1998) developed into complicated compliance systems that few teachers really understood, and a diversity of focus that furthered the aims of those with philosophical agendas or products to sell. The revised National Curriculum of 2007 was vague, and the knowledge component was downplayed. 'Personal Learning and Thinking Skills' were introduced. So were the 'Four deeps'. Students donned Edward de Bono's thinking hats, pressed their brain buttons and completed learning styles questionnaires. Despite superficially sub-scribing to many progressive preoccupations, such as a focus on the individual, these innovations resembled less a principled philosophy and more a symphony played on kazoos.

Conclusion

The purpose of this chapter has not been to provide a comprehensive history of education, but to equip you with some context to help you understand the ideas that you will encounter in the rest of this book and in your teaching career. Although the term 'innovation' is usually used positively in schools and at education conferences, it is often used inaccurately. Much of what is considered innovative today can be traced back through time. It is only because we have a strangely ahis-torical profession that such claims can go unexamined. It is clear from the experience of England, that simply investing more money in edu-cation will not necessarily deliver an improved quality of education.

Increased spending may be desirable but there is a moral imperative to ensure that additional money is spent on initiatives that will have a positive impact rather than on innovations that sound plausible, promise much, but deliver little.

References

Ashman, G., 2017. Learning lessons from the failure of Scotland's 'Curriculum for Excellence'. [Blog] *Filling the Pail*. Available at: https://gregashman.wordpress.com/2017/03/22/learning-lessons-from-the-failure-of-scotlands-curriculum-for-excellence/.

Austin, L.M., 2003. Children of childhood: nostalgia and the romantic legacy. *Studies in Romanticism*, 42(1), pp. 75–98.

Australian Curriculum, 2018. *Australian Curriculum*, version 8.3 [online]. Available at: http://australiancurriculum.edu.au.

Babbitt, F., trans., 1927. *Plutarch Moralia Volume 1*. Cambridge, MA: Harvard University Press/Loeb Classical Library.

Bestor, A., 1953. *Educational Wastelands*. Urbana: University of Illinois Press.

Biesta, G., 2015. *The Beautiful Risk of Education*. Abingdon: Routledge.

Black, P. and Wiliam, D., 1998. *Inside the Black Box: Raising Standards through Classroom Assessment*. London: GL Assessment.

Bobbitt, J., 1918. *The Curriculum*. Boston, MA: Houghton Mifflin.

Central Advisory Council for Education, 1967. *Children and their Primary Schools* (The Plowden Report). London: Her Majesty's Stationery Office. Available at: http://www.educationengland.org.uk/documents/plowden/plowden1967-1.html.

Chowdry, H. and Sibieta, L., 2011. *Trends in Education and Schools Spending*. London: Institute for Fiscal Studies.

Coe, R., 2013. *Improving Education: A Triumph of Hope Over Experience*. Durham, NC: Centre for Evaluation and Monitoring, Durham University.

Dewey, J., 1902. *The Child and the Curriculum*. Chicago, IL: University of Chicago Press.

Dewey, J., 1913. *Interest and Effort in Education*. Boston, MA: Houghton Mifflin.

Dewey, J., 1938. Experience and education. *The Kappa Delta Pi Lecture Series*. New York: Collier Books.

Duffus, R., 1953. Education and the way it's Practiced: QUACKERY IN THE PUBLIC SCHOOLS, by Albert Lynd. *New York Times*, 13 September.

Egan, K., 1980. John Dewey and the social studies curriculum. *Theory & Research in Social Education*, 8(2), pp. 37–55.

Egan, K., 2002. *Getting It Wrong from the Beginning: Our Progressivist Inheritance from Spencer, Herbert and Piaget*. New Haven, CT: Yale University Press.

Flesch, R., 1955. *Why Johnny Can't Read And What You Can Do About It*. New York: Harpers.

Galton, M., 1987. An ORACLE chronicle: A decade of classroom research. *Teaching and Teacher Education*, *3*(4), pp. 299–313.

Gore, J., Lloyd, A., Smith, M., Bowe, J., Ellis, H. and Lubans, D., 2017. Effects of professional development on the quality of teaching: results from a randomised controlled trial of Quality Teaching Rounds. *Teaching and Teacher Education*, *68*, pp. 99–113.

Hirsch, E.D., 2016. *Why Knowledge Matters: Rescuing Our Children from Failed Educational Theories*. Cambridge, MA: Harvard Education Press.

Jackson, M., 2012. Plato (429–347 BC), in N.M. Seel (eds), *Encyclopedia of the Sciences of Learning*. Boston, MA: Springer.

Kamii, C. and Dominick, A., 1998. The harmful effects of algorithms in grades 1–4, in L.J. Morrow and M.J. Kenney (eds), *The Teaching and Learning of Algorithms in School Mathematics*: 1998 NCTM Yearbook. Reston, VA: National Council of Teachers of Mathematics. pp. 130–40.

Kilpatrick, W.H., 1918. *The Project Method: The Use of the Purposeful Act in the Educative Process* (No. 3). New York: Teachers College, Columbia University.

Krahenbuhl, K.S., 2016. Student-centered education and constructivism: challenges, concerns, and clarity for teachers. *The Clearing House: A Journal of Educational Strategies, Issues and Ideas*, *89*(3), pp. 97–105.

Kuhs, T.M. and Flake, C.L., 1993. Lighting the flame: constructivism and teacher education. *Journal of Early Childhood Teacher Education*, *4*(3), pp. 4–8.

Life, 1958. Crisis in education. *Life*, 24 March.

Lingard, R.L., Ladwig, J., Mills, M.D., Hayes, D., Luke, A., Gore, J. and Christie, P.H., 2001. *The Queensland School Reform Longitudinal Study*, Volume 1. Brisbane: State of Queensland Department of Education.

Lynd, A., 1953. *Quackery in the Public Schools*. Little, Brown.

MacLeod, A.S., 1992. From rational to romantic: the children of children's literature in the nineteenth century. *Poetics Today*, *13*(1), pp. 141–53.

Mayer, R.E., 2004. Should there be a three-strikes rule against pure discovery learning? *American Psychologist*, *59*(1), pp. 14–19.

Mayo, P., 2014. Gramsci and the politics of education. *Capital & Class*, *38*(2), pp. 385–98.

McNaught, K. and Berlach, R.G., 2007. Outcomes based education?: Rethinking the provision of compulsory education in Western Australia. *Issues in Educational Research*, *17*(1), p. 1.

O'Toole, G., 2013 *The Mind Is Not a Vessel that Needs Filling, but Wood that Needs Igniting*. [online] Available at: https://quoteinvestigator.com/2013/03/28/mind-fire/.

Paul, R. and Elder, L., 2007. Critical thinking: the art of Socratic questioning. *Journal of Developmental Education*, *31*(1), p. 36.

Perkins, D., 1999. The many faces of constructivism. *Educational Leadership*, *57*(3), pp. 6–11.

Ravitch, D., 2000. Left back. *A Century of Battles Over School Reform*. New York: Touchstone.

Reynolds, D. and Muijs, D., 1999. The effective teaching of mathematics: a review of research. *School Leadership & Management*, 19(3), pp. 273–88.

Robinson, K., 2017. Sir Ken Robinson on how schools are stifling students' creativity. Interviewed by D.I. Peritz, *The Globe and Mail*, 7 September. [online] Available at: https://beta.theglobeandmail.com/news/national/education/sir-ken-robinson-on-how-schools-are-stifling-students-crea tivity/article36205832/?ref=http://www.theglobeandmail.com&.

Rosenow, E., 1980. Rousseau's Emile, an Anti-Utopia. *British Journal of Educational Studies*, 28(3), pp. 212–24.

Rutherford, F.J., 1997. Sputnik and science education, in Symposium 'Reflecting on Sputnik: Linking the Past, Present, and Future of Educational Reform'. Washington, DC.

Smith, M.B., 1950. *And Madly Teach: A Layman Looks at Public School Education*. Chicago, IL: Henry Regnery Company.

2

CLASSROOM MANAGEMENT

Key Points

This chapter will:

- Define classroom management
- Explain the tools available for managing classrooms; strategies, routines and policies
- Give practical examples of strategies, routines and policies and how to put these into practice

What is good classroom management?

Classroom management may be defined as the set of strategies, routines and policies that teachers and schools employ in order to maximise the amount of lesson time that students spend thinking about and working with academic content. Such a definition is inherently controversial and requires us to accept the goal of maximising academic engagement. Some would argue differently, suggesting that interweaving social and academic talk does not detract from student learning (see Horn and Campbell, 2015, for example). Nevertheless, convincing evidence from a large body of research suggests that the greater the amount of academic learning time, the more effective the learning environment (Brophy, 1986).

In my experience, new teachers invariably prioritise good classroom management and worry about losing control. There are some indications that standard approaches to teacher training are deficient with respect to classroom management (O'Neill and Stephenson, 2014; Carter, 2015) and I suspect that this is due to a distaste for the type of 'behaviourist' research that often has the most to tell new teachers about how to improve classroom behaviour (Emmer and Stough, 2001).

Even experienced teachers, myself included, sometimes have 'the teacher dream' where they are standing at the front of a class, ineffectually issuing instructions as students completely ignore these edicts and chaos reigns.

So let's acknowledge these concerns but reframe them so that we may productively address them. Classroom management is not simply about managing poor behaviour; it is as much about creating conditions that will *prevent* behaviour problems from developing in the first place (see e.g. Glynn, 1982 on antecedent control of behaviour). Many new teachers have gone to observe an experienced colleague with a reputation for good classroom management, only to leave that observation baffled, complaining that the experienced teacher did not appear to be doing *anything* to manage the behaviour of the class – behaviour that was, nonetheless, perfect.

At this point, it is worth noting a cognitive bias known as the 'Fundamental Attribution Error' (Ross, 1977). If someone cuts in front of you in traffic then you might think, 'What a selfish person!' or words to that effect. You might even be tempted to make predictions about their future behaviour on this basis. Yet when *you* cut in front of others in traffic it is because you are late for an appointment or you are distracted by your children having an argument in the back of the car. This demonstrates our tendency to attribute the behaviour of others to deep personality traits while attributing our own behaviour to circumstance. The fact that many classroom behaviour problems may be prevented by creating the right conditions demonstrates that behaviour *is* influenced a great deal by circumstance and so we need to bear this in mind when dealing with the behaviour of young people.

We also need to recognise that control is not the objective. Students will often talk of teachers who can or cannot 'control' the class and so this creeps into our vernacular. But the objective is, and must always be, to maximise academic learning time. Control for the sake of control is simply authoritarianism and is open to justifiable criticism. It conjures visions of the kinds of abuses in some schools and children's homes that we have seen exposed in recent years.

The tools of classroom management

I will draw a distinction between strategies, routines and policies. Strategies are the kind of moment-by-moment decisions that teachers make about how to interact with students. These could almost be termed 'skills' because, after a lot of practice, experienced teachers will start to deploy them without conscious thought. The fact that some teachers seem to intuitively sense which strategies to employ does not mean that these cannot be learnt and effectively deployed by teachers who do not possess this intuition.

Routines are mostly preventative and are designed to habituate appropriate behaviour. For instance, a teacher might require students to start work on a 'starter' activity as soon as they enter the room. If this happens every lesson, then students will become used to it and most will engage automatically. This will have the effect of halting conversations that were taking place in the corridor and that might otherwise have caused disruption to the start of the lesson. Such routines take time to build and this is why the new teacher who drops in to lesson number seventeen is unable to observe the work that went into setting-up these routines, only the seemingly effortless result.

Policies are essentially 'If … then …' statements. For instance, if a student does not complete homework then what will happen? Or, if a student persistently does not follow a teacher's instructions then what will happen? In my view, these are best tackled at a whole-school level but many schools do not adopt a clear approach. In schools that do not, teachers effectively engineer their own policies, which then rub up against, and sometimes jar with, the policies of other teachers and the ideas of senior managers within the school, creating an overall system of culture and practice. This can lead to incoherence. Students are particularly alert to perceived injustice and so they will tend to react negatively if they think different teachers are applying different standards.

Sometimes, it may not be clear that a policy issue rests with a school rather than a teacher until there is a conflict. For instance, imagine that a teacher decides to rearrange the seating in her Year 3 class so that the students are seated in rows, and that a parent then complains about this to the principal who decides that the tables must be moved back to a group position. The teacher will feel undermined and so, for this reason, it is wise for schools to have clearly articulated policies and for new teachers to always run these kinds of ideas past senior staff before proceeding.

As a new teacher, there is one concept that you should be particularly wary of, especially if expressed by a senior member of staff. I would go as far as to suggest that you might want to avoid accepting a teaching post in a school where this belief is prevalent. You may even wish to ask a few 'If … then …' questions in order to figure this out. The concept is expressed well by Randy Hitz, when he suggests that '[t]he best way to prevent [inappropriate] behaviour is to provide stimulating, developmentally appropriate activities' (Hitz, 1988).

There is little evidence that such a statement is true. It may be the case that allowing students to draw a picture rather than write a passage will lead to more short-term compliance but it does not maximise academic learning. Rather, it reduces the academic experience of students who display behaviour problems.

The idea also seems implausible from a theoretical perspective. It relies on the ability of an interesting task to lead to intrinsic motivation – students who are self-motivated – which will, in turn, be sufficient to militate against all of the other factors that might prompt students to misbehave. We will explore the idea of motivation in Chapter 4.

The concept that poor behaviour is caused by poor teaching can lead to a situation where senior staff avoid their responsibility for a damaging whole-school culture by claiming that it is the fault of individual teachers when students misbehave. This philosophy may prompt teachers to plan ever more entertaining lessons, only for those lessons to be derailed when students do not even allow a teacher to explain the motivating activities that she has prepared. Indeed, teacher burnout due to an inability to deal with behaviour problems seems to be a key reason why teachers leave the profession (Aloe et al., 2014).

As we will see in the next chapter, education is not an exact science where we know precisely what will happen if we push a certain button or pull a specific lever. Research into behaviour management strategies is particularly difficult because of the possibility of expectation effects, that is, the way that teachers' and students' expectations of the value of the strategy influence how they behave and also influence the way they tend to report its results on instruments such as surveys. Nevertheless, there are studies of whole-school approaches such as School-Wide Positive Behaviour Interventions and Supports (SWPBIS) that seem to show promise (Bradshaw et al., 2010).

Robert Marzano and colleagues have approached the problem using meta-analysis, summarising the results of many studies, in order to try to draw-out underlying principles, as well as relying on other research such as studies that record the behaviours of more successful teachers (Marzano et al., 2003). Individual approaches focused around teacher professional development also appear to make a difference (Wheldall, 1991). Taken together, the evidence is strong enough to suggest some effective methods.

These methods generally take a 'behaviourist' stance – a carrot-and-stick approach with a heavy emphasis on the carrots. There are those who argue that punishments and rewards only ever lead to short-term compliance. For instance, some contend that rewards undermine intrinsic motivation (Deci et al., 1999). Others argue that this depends upon the nature of the reward, with verbal rewards or praise being more benign (Cameron et al., 2001). Overall, there appears to be strong evidence for the utility of behaviourist approaches (Gable et al., 2009).

Perhaps it is not a case of choosing one or the other. Perhaps we can orient students towards academic learning by initially using a behaviourist approach and, once they have developed capacity and a sense of accomplishment, self-motivation will come.

The remainder of this chapter will focus first on strategies, then routines, and finally look at behaviour policies that may or may not be enacted at the whole-school level.

Strategies

Specific strategies that teachers use in the classroom to manage behaviour have been observed through process–product research. This type of research places observers in classrooms to record teacher behaviours and then see if particular behaviours correlate to gains in students' academic performance (Brophy and Good, 1984).

There are whole-school programmes that have shown some success, which include training in specific strategies. An example of such a programme is Assertive Discipline, developed by Lee Canter in 1979 (Tauber, 1999). Researchers have also worked with teachers to train them in behavioural principles, often known as 'Positive Teaching', with some marked successes on subsequent classroom behaviour (for example, Wheldall, 1991).

Synthesising the advice from these programmes, a number of approaches emerge, alongside others that may only suit a particular place and time or phase of teaching. What follows is a list of common strategies that you may wish to experiment with in your own classrooms. Many of them sound like simple common sense but the key is enacting them in a planned and purposeful way, something that requires considerable deliberate practice.

Be assertive and stay calm. The notion of being 'assertive' rather than 'passive' or 'hostile' was popularised by Assertive Discipline and is quite useful in thinking about classroom management. Passive teachers plead with their classes: '*Please* be quiet!' Hostile teachers show aggression: 'I have *told* you to be quiet! What part of '*be quiet*' do you not understand?' Assertive teachers take a more neutral, factual tone: 'I am waiting for quiet before I begin,' while remaining warm and friendly.

There are a number of reasons why an assertive approach is best. It signals that you are in control. If you lose your temper then not only are you modelling poor behaviour, to some extent you are also giving students a gossip-worthy reward. Focusing on the facts, the observable behaviours, helps reduce the emotional heat. It is easier to stay calm if you do two things: place some distance between yourself and your role and have a plan for what to do next. I used to imagine that 'the teacher' was a puppet under my control, I could experiment with what the teacher did and see how the students responded. This helps when students inevitably say hurtful things that they don't really mean. They are reacting to 'the teacher' and not to you as an individual.

A variant of the neutral approach is to acknowledge, but not reward, unhelpful comments. If a student declares, 'this lesson is really boring,' then ignoring this comment might prompt the student to repeat it whereas challenging the comment might open the door to an argument. Instead, a good response might be to say, 'I understand that this is how you feel. Please complete the questions.' It leaves the student with nowhere to go. Similarly, you may choose to tactically ignore some minor infringements in order to prevent students gaining the reward of your attention (Gable et al., 2009). This does, of course, depend on the culture of your school.

Teach behaviour; don't assume. More effective teachers take time at the start of the year to teach students what they want them to do, which they then follow-up with monitoring and correction (Emmer and Stough, 2001). Many new teachers assume that students will know what is expected but the reality is that teachers vary greatly in their expectations. Couple this with the fact that students are not always conscious of their own behaviours and the need for clear and explicit instructions becomes obvious.

If you have a set of rules then you need to teach your students these rules. This is aided by ensuring that there are only about four or five broad rules (Gable et al., 2009).

Manage proximity: Generally, you should aim to position yourself so that you can see as much of the classroom as possible. One way is to stand at the front of the room but you can also stand at the back. This can be particularly effective if the students are seated in rows and you want them to pay attention to something that is written or projected at the front of the room.

If a student is engaged in fairly minor misbehaviour, then simply walking towards that student is often enough to prompt him to stop. If not, you are now in a position to talk privately to him (see below).

Positive reinforcement, or 'Catch them being good': Imagine you are teaching a class of 26 students arranged in rows. You have asked them all to write a paragraph in their books. Two students in the middle row have not yet put pen to paper and, instead, seem to be having a conversation. What do you do?

The instinctive response is to criticise the two students who are not completing the work and this appears to be what many teachers do (Beaman and Wheldall, 2000). But there are two drawbacks to this. First, you create a situation of conflict where the students may not want to back down. They may start to think of reasons why they were not completing the task and enunciate these. Second, you have now highlighted to the 24 students who are following your instructions that some students are not. Do they need to know this? It perhaps diminishes your authority.

An alternative might be to say, 'Excellent everyone on the front row; good to see you are getting on with this. Good work everyone on the back row; it's great to see you writing your paragraphs.' You can do this whilst moving around the room, ostensibly *noticing this good work*. It is important to *praise the behaviour and be specific about this* rather than generally praising the individuals.

Often, the two students on the middle row will get the hint and start working. They are much more likely to comply because they have not become personally invested in the not-writing-a-paragraph position. All being well, by the time you make your way back to the middle row, you can comment on the fact that they are all writing the paragraph too.

Criticise privately, wherever possible: It is better to reinforce behaviours positively but sometimes you will need to admonish a student or warn her of a possible consequence if a behaviour continues. Again, it is important to be specific about the behaviour that you wish to see her change and it is best to provide this criticism privately. You do not want an audience because then your interactions become more of a performance. Publicly criticising a student can be humiliating and foster resentment.

For minor matters, you may simply approach a student and have a quiet word. If you think that the discussion will be more prolonged, then you can ask the student to briefly leave the room so that you may talk to him outside the door. If you do this, you need to ensure that you can still monitor the rest of the class, perhaps through a window in the door or by leaving it ajar. It is also surprisingly easy to forget about the student and leave him standing outside for 5 minutes or more so deal with him straight away.

Sometimes, you may find that you ask a student to leave the room and she refuses to do so. A useful approach is to *use repeated instructions that focus on the desired behaviour*. For instance, imagine the following dialogue:

> *Teacher:*   Please leave the room, I would like to discuss this with you outside.
>
> *Student:*   But it wasn't me; it was Carlo who was throwing the paper!
>
> *Teacher:*   Please leave the room, I would like to talk to you about this outside.
>
> *Student:*   Why aren't you speaking to Carlo? He was the one who threw the paper!
>
> *Teacher:*   We can discuss this outside. Please leave the room.

Many students will comply by the time that you have issued three such instructions but if a student does not, then simply state something like, 'OK, we will discuss this at lunch,' and move on.

Frame consequences as choices: One objective of teaching students the behaviours that you expect is to develop their agency. Students need to feel in control of their own behaviour if they are to attempt to modify it. Consider a teacher making two statements to a student that effectively mean the same thing:

- Statement 1: 'If you keep rocking on your chair like that then I'm going to keep you behind at the start of lunch.'
- Statement 2: 'If you choose to continue rocking on your chair then you will be choosing to stay behind at the start of lunch.'

The first statement is more personal and implies that it is the teacher who has agency. The second statement implies that it is the student who is making choices. It is also a lot harder to argue with.

Follow through: There is, of course, little value in stating that you will discuss an issue with a student during lunch if you then don't follow through with this. It is better not to state a consequence than to state a consequence that you don't enforce. This will simply teach your students that you don't mean what you say.

Occasionally you might issue a consequence that you later realise you do not want to enforce. Perhaps you have a lunch duty or perhaps you overreacted. Rather than simply letting it slip, it is better to be up front about this: 'I said that I would see you here at lunch but I had forgotten about my lunch duty – we will pick this up tomorrow instead,' or, 'I've thought about it and decided that an after school detention is too harsh. However, I do expect to see an improvement in your behaviour tomorrow.' In my view, it is better to admit that you were wrong than to simply neglect a consequence.

Take account of school culture and use the right language: Schools can be odd places and words that have a certain meaning in one school will have a different meaning in another. In my present school a 'detention' is a very formal thing that takes place on a Friday and is only given for quite serious infringements. However, keeping a student back at the start of recess to discuss an issue or asking a student to return at lunch to complete work are consequences that are not considered to be 'detentions' because they are restorative approaches that are designed to address the original issue. However, in other schools, keeping students back during breaks might be called 'detentions'. It is important to get a handle on this in any new school.

Consider how you present yourself – be an actor if necessary: If a particular class offers behaviour challenges, then it can be hard to smile and be warm and friendly. Yet it is worth trying, even if this is an act. Even in the most difficult class, there will be many students who have done nothing wrong and deserve your approval. By smiling you signal that you feel in control, which will help students to believe that you *are* in control. Friendliness aids with the mission of making positive comments – something that is hard to do with a nervous or pained look on your face.

'No dark sarcasm in the classroom': Humour can work extremely well, building a bond between teacher and students. Yet there are two traps that new teachers fall into that are best avoided: making fun of a student and/or using sarcasm. Some experienced teachers *can* get away with this because they have developed a long track-record that means students give them the benefit of the doubt; they know that the teacher cares and has their best interests at heart. But it is still

very risky and there are experienced teachers who use sarcasm and belittling who unnecessarily hurt and demoralise students.

Sarcasm is structurally difficult because it involves saying something that is the opposite of what you mean. Students are still learning and are often not on the same page. The potential for misunderstanding is large and, if they *do* misunderstand, then they get the opposite of the intended message rather than a meaningless or absurd one. This is why I favour absurdist humour – think Monty Python. It is pretty hard to miss the message that it is *intended* to be funny, even if it is not.

Be controlled and strategic about releasing personal information: Humour is an aspect of your personality and you will want to share some personal information over time in order to better relate to your students. The key is to keep control and be strategic. Questions such as 'Do you have a boyfriend?' or 'Are you gay?' should be met with an unflustered, assertive, 'That is not relevant to the task we are completing'. Your love life is unlikely to ever be an appropriate thing to discuss, bar engagement or a wedding. However, you might want to drop in a favourite sporting team or a pastime that you enjoy. But make sure that *you* decide when to do this and, in order to be certain that it reinforces good behaviour on the part of the students, select a time when the class has just worked well and completed the tasks that you have set with the minimum of disruption.

Political and religious beliefs are troublesome. Clearly, teachers are not employed to evangelise or indoctrinate and this leads many to conclude that such views should not be shared at all. However, if asked directly by an older student, I will tend to disclose my beliefs. This is a moral dilemma. On the one hand, by sharing these beliefs it could be argued that I am promoting them. On the other hand, if I don't disclose them then how can a student evaluate the potential for bias in the way that I have taught something such as the Big Bang theory?

Routines

Routines can act to prevent behaviour problems from arising. If a student has to do something every lesson, then it will develop into a habit that he or she does not need to think about. The routines outlined in this section could form part of a whole-school behaviour policy but, if not, they are relatively simple to implement as an individual teacher.

Start academic learning from the beginning of the lesson: The start of the lesson sets the scene for what will continue. If students are essentially hanging around while you get things ready then they are likely to continue chatting about issues that they have brought into the classroom from outside. If possible, and it is *not* always possible, arrive at your class early, set everything up and have a worthwhile activity for students to start as soon as they enter the room, perhaps a recap of something from a previous lesson (Rosenshine, 2012) that is relevant for today but that they can tackle independently. I have sometimes found that, if I do this, some students will also start to arrive early. In this instance, I give them a pre-starter, a task that is supplementary to the official starter activity but that is, again, educationally worthwhile.

Some teachers attempt to start the lesson well by lining-up students outside the classroom door. While this can work well, I have also seen this strategy lead to considerable disorder in narrow corridors or where students from other classes interact with the students who are lining-up.

Have a seating plan: It is always easier to connect with a student if you use the student's name. Seating plans help you to learn names when you first teach a new class. If *you* design the plan, rather than simply recording where students have chosen to sit, then you also demonstrate that your classroom is a place for learning rather than socialising. I am sure that many children are relieved when a teacher takes charge of the seating because it gives them respite from social pressures.

You might also want to consider alternating genders. Again, this disrupts many of the natural social groupings that would otherwise arise. Sometimes, a group of boys can start to dominate the classroom while a group of quieter girls is largely forgotten.

There is considerable evidence that seating students in rows facing the teacher is preferable to seating them in groups. A circle or semi-circle arrangement where everyone can see everyone else may be particularly good for whole-class discussions although it is an inefficient use of space and so will not work with large classes (Wheldall and Bradd, 2013).

Seating students in groups has become ubiquitous in English primary schools since the publication of the Plowden Report in the 1960s (Galton, 1987). The original intention was to encourage different kinds of teaching and yet, despite the widespread change in seating arrangements, teachers still tend to use a lot of whole-class teaching, and with good reason (Miao et al., 2015). This means that many students will have their backs to the teacher and will be facing a peer who may be a source of distraction.

It may not be within your authority to change seating arrangements so you should check that out with your school leadership if this is something that you are considering.

Direct questions to specific students: Questioning students serves a number of purposes, including obtaining information about their level of understanding. It also acts as a routine that ensures academic engagement. Unfortunately, many teachers do not take advantage of this.

The key principle is that students should not be able to predict whether they will be asked to respond. If a teacher organises a class so that only those students who raise their hands will be asked to respond, the students can tune-out, safe in the knowledge that they will not be asked a question. Some teachers introduce a 'no-hands' rule so that students are not permitted to raise their hands. They might also use randomisers – for instance, a teacher might write each student's name on a piece of paper and then draw them at random. It is not necessary to go this far as long as you do not ask just those students who have their hands raised and you have a mechanism for ensuring that you get to everybody, such as ticking each child's name on a class list once you've asked a question.

Better still, you might introduce mechanisms that allow you to *question all students* simultaneously. For example, students might write their answers on a mini-whiteboard, raise thumbs-up for true and thumbs-down for false to a true/false question, or use A, B, C, D cards to signal their responses to a multiple-choice question. You cannot really ask for long and sophisticated responses this way but you can require a response from every single student in the class and this means that they will all need to pay attention.

It is worth practising the way that you do this. For instance, with mini-whiteboards I use a 'think ... and ... show' routine. During the thinking time no student is allowed to raise their mini-whiteboard and then when I say 'show' they are all expected to do so at the same time. I make a point of insisting on this when I first train a class in the routine, otherwise students might change their answers based upon the other answers that they see.

Dylan Wiliam has documented a number of such routines (Wiliam, 2011) and we will examine the assessment evidence that they provide to teachers in more detail in Chapter 8.

Make attention visible: Teachers face the same problem, again and again in slightly different contexts. The stuff that we are trying to change – the contents of students' minds – is actually invisible and we can only really infer what is going on by proxies. How do we know if a student is paying attention? We can ask a question or we can set up other visible routines that might help.

One approach is to ensure that students are tracking the teacher when he is speaking to the class. This is an element of Doug Lemov's 'SLANT' strategy. SLANT stands for Sit up, Listen, Ask and answer questions, Nod your head and Track the teacher (Lemov, 2010). Yes, a student can be listening while staring out the window and a student can be tracking you and nodding while thinking about last night's football match. But you are playing the odds here. You are maximising the *chance* that students are paying attention.

Another strategy that accomplishes this same aim is for use when the whole class is intended to be reading a text together. It is an idea I learnt from blogger and languages teacher Barry Smith (Smith, 2016). Simply ask students to place a ruler under the line of text as it is being read. It is then pretty easy to see if students are keeping up and following the text.

Policies

Many schools will have a code of conduct but this alone is not a policy if it just consists of a list of rules. These may be framed positively – 'treat teachers and other students with respect' – but they are simply a list of assertions rather than the kind of, 'If ... then ...' statements that have practical value.

All schools have some kind of a policy but these will vary in their explicitness. Some school behaviour policies will be clear and open. For instance, a particularly draconian policy might suggest that a student who is misbehaving in class, as defined by breaking one of the school rules, be issued with a warning and if they continue to misbehave then the teacher is expected to call for a patrolling staff member to escort the student away to a withdrawal room.

In many schools, the policy is far more implicit and consists of a set of accepted practices that have been built over time as part of the school culture. This will result in considerable variation in how behaviour issues are dealt with. The policy will not be clear.

The worst of situations is to have a contradictory mix of the two: a school with an explicit policy that the culture suggests you are *not* supposed to follow. For instance, in some schools, you might follow the policy to the letter and call for the patrolling teacher, only for this to be seen as a sign that you are not effective at managing behaviour or that you teach uninspiring lessons. It is critical that you are aware of both the letter of your school's behaviour policy and of the culture and practice that surrounds it.

However, it is perfectly reasonable for your school to ask you to document your decisions and you should not view such a request as an attempt to stop you using the behaviour policy. Filling in a form or logging an incident on a computer is essential to allowing information to flow around the school. Otherwise, you cannot expect a school leader to notice patterns of behaviour. When logging incidents, you should always make it clear whether you are simply passing on information or are expecting further action. If not, you might become frustrated and so might your colleagues.

Some policies will be poorly designed. For instance, schools often ask teachers to write students' names on the board as a warning yet, for some students, this could well act as a perverse incentive.

What of the school where Stage 2 of the policy is a one-hour detention and Stage 3 is withdrawal from class? A student on Stage 2 is likely to conclude that withdrawal from class is preferable to a detention and so continue to misbehave in order to move to Stage 3.

Many school policies are also quite flat. There is one approach and, once it has been exhausted, there is nothing more. This results in seeing the same students in detention or attracting the same sanction repeatedly, with no sign of improvement.

A student who cannot behave appropriately in a classroom needs a specific intervention. If a child cannot read then we would wish to provide explicit teaching in reading and perhaps withdraw that child from other lessons in order to be able to deliver this. Similarly, a student who is not able to behave in a socially acceptable way will also need an explicit intervention. Often, we might require both kinds of intervention for a given student because a failure to learn to read is likely to lead to broader academic disengagement.

However, such an intervention is the *opposite* of giving a child 'time-out' where standards of behaviour are dropped. This implies that socially acceptable behaviour is somehow special and is not expected of everybody all the time. It illustrates the key tension between accommodating a student's difficulty and addressing it.

If a student is blind, we would not ask them to read regular books. They can't. And so we would accommodate this disability. We might give them an audiobook to listen to or a braille version of the book. If a student demonstrates poor behaviour and we conclude that this is due to a disability, then we might also be tempted to accommodate this and hold different expectations of their behaviour. Sometimes, this may be appropriate; for example, a child could be suffering from a neurological disorder. However, in many cases, much can be done to address behaviour issues, even for students with conditions such as autism (Wong et al., 2015). So simply lowering our expectations might not be the right thing to do.

A whole-school approach that operates on several layers of intervention and for which we have some empirical evidence is School-Wide Positive Behaviour Interventions and Supports (SWPBIS). A number of randomised controlled trials have been conducted on the effectiveness of schools implementing SWPBIS and these generally show a drop in disruptive behaviours (Bradshaw et al., 2010) with hints that students who benefit most are those who are most at risk (Bradshaw et al., 2015).

SWPBIS is more of a framework than a completely specified programme. A key part of the design is to build capacity within schools to develop their own systems with external support. A team of staff is selected who draw up a list of three to five whole-school positively stated behaviour expectations such as, 'Be respectful, responsible, and ready to learn,' which are then posted in all rooms. These expectations are explicitly taught to students, with teachers developing lesson plans to do this. A school system of rewards and negative consequences is devised. Rewards include simple acknowledgements rather than necessarily being tangible (Bradshaw et al., 2010).

There are also additional tiers of support. Data is collected on disciplinary issues and this is used to help decide upon interventions such as, 'study skills groups, check in/check out, social skills groups, and dropout prevention programs', as well as the highest tier of individualised support (Flannery and Kato, 2016).

If you do not have the support of a system such as this, or even one that encompasses some of these elements, then it is possible to try to adapt these principles to your own classes. In many schools, teachers may set detentions and yet it is not clearly defined as to what these are for. So develop a system of rules with your classes and then explain what will trigger a detention.

You should also include positive rewards as part of your system, and these are not the same as the simple acknowledgements that I advised earlier. They are more formal. American programmes often advocate rewarding students with something like a 'high-five', which, to outsiders, may seem quite culturally specific. I have found that a little pre-printed note or certificate that a student can take home or, for something more significant, a phone call home, will be appreciated by students. Avoid the tendency to reward only those students who have reformed rather than those students who *always* behave appropriately.

One whole-class reward that I have used successfully in science teaching is to give students a 10-minute slot to ask me any question they wish about science. The students are required to accept that I might rule a question inappropriate or that I might not know the answer. However, I will otherwise do my best to address the question. I particularly like this approach because it rewards the students with science rather than something extraneous.

When it comes to negative consequences, it is a good idea to have a graduated, stepwise response. At each step, further sanctions should be presented as a choice and discussions about them should be held as privately as possible. Rather than writing students' names on the board, I would advise annotating a class list. If necessary, have a pen and a clipboard with the list attached ready for use.

A progressive system of consequences that I have used is:

1. Warning
2. Quiet word outside the classroom door
3. Short detention (10 minutes at break or lunch)
4. Long detention (40 minutes after school)

As 'Step 5', I would ask for withdrawal from an on-call teacher and ensure that the student still completed the 40-minute detention. Although it should be rarely used, this step depends upon what is possible at a whole-school level. If there really is no last resort like this available, then I would question whether this is the right school in which to begin your teaching career.

Putting it into practice

As with other aspects of teaching, classroom management is a complex skill. Initially, the experience is similar to learning to drive; there are just too many things to remember to do and, moreover, you also have to teach the lesson content at the same time. You cannot expect to employ all of the strategies that I have listed from your first moment of teaching. Routines can be planned in advance and established early, saving you lots of attention later on, and so a key focus of the first few lessons is to ensure these routines have taken hold. And rest assured that, just as in learning to drive, actions that you initially have to consciously think about will soon become automatic and you can focus on the reason why you are there: to teach.

Conclusion

Classroom management is an essential skill. It is the foundation of all other classroom teaching skills and it is an area that new teachers find difficult. We can draw on 'behaviourist' research to help establish the best approaches to classroom management. However, it is a complex issue that also requires the application of a fair amount of craft knowledge. I have defined three aspects to classroom management: strategies, routines and policies. A particularly important aspect is the use of routines to prevent issues from arising in the first place. The level of control a classroom teacher has over each of the aspects of the classroom, and kinds of approaches that are considered acceptable, will be determined by school culture. It is therefore essential to understand the culture of a school before accepting a teaching position.

References

Aloe, A.M., Amo, L.C. and Shanahan, M.E., 2014. Classroom management self-efficacy and burnout: a multivariate meta-analysis. *Educational Psychology Review*, 26(1), pp.101–26.

Beaman, R. and Wheldall, K., 2000. Teachers' use of approval and disapproval in the classroom. *Educational Psychology*, 20(4), pp. 431–46.

Bradshaw, C.P., Mitchell, M.M. and Leaf, P.J., 2010. Examining the effects of schoolwide positive behavioral interventions and supports on student outcomes results from a randomized controlled effectiveness trial in elementary schools. *Journal of Positive Behavior Interventions*, 12(3), pp. 133–48.

Bradshaw, C.P., Waasdorp, T.E. and Leaf, P.J., 2015. Examining variation in the impact of school-wide positive behavioral interventions and supports: findings from a randomized controlled effectiveness trial. *Journal of Educational Psychology*, 107(2), p. 546.

Brophy, J., 1986. Teacher influences on student achievement. *American Psychologist*, 41(10), p. 1069.

Brophy, J.E. and Good, T.L., 1984. *Teacher Behavior and Student Achievement*. No. 73. East Lansing, MI: Institute for Research on Teaching, Michigan State University.

Cameron, J., Banko, K.M. and Pierce, W.D., 2001. Pervasive negative effects of rewards on intrinsic motivation: the myth continues. *The Behavior Analyst*, 24(1), p. 1.

Carter, A., 2015. *Carter Review of Initial Teacher Training (ITT)*. London: Department for Education. DFE-00036-2015. Available at: www.gov.uk/government/publications/carter-review-of-initial-teacher-training.

Deci, E.L., Koestner, R. and Ryan, R.M., 1999. A meta-analytic review of experiments examining the effects of extrinsic rewards on intrinsic motivation. *Psychological Bulletin*, 125(6), p. 627.

Emmer, E.T. and Stough, L.M., 2001. Classroom management: a critical part of educational psychology, with implications for teacher education. *Educational Psychologist*, 36(2), pp. 103–12.

Flannery, K.B. and Kato, M.M., 2016. Implementation of SWPBIS in high school: why is it different? *Preventing School Failure: Alternative Education for Children and Youth*, pp. 1–8.

Gable, R.A., Hester, P.H., Rock, M.L. and Hughes, K.G., 2009. Back to basics rules, praise, ignoring, and reprimands revisited. *Intervention in School and Clinic*, 44(4), pp. 195–205.

Galton, M., 1987. Change and continuity in the primary school: the research evidence. *Oxford Review of Education*, 13(1), pp. 81–93.

Glynn, T., 1982. Antecedent control of behaviour in educational contexts. *Educational Psychology*, 2(3–4), pp. 215–29.

Hitz, R., 1988. Assertive discipline: a response to Lee Canter. *Young Children*, 43(2), pp. 25–6.

Horn, I.S. and Campbell, S.S., 2015. Developing pedagogical judgment in novice teachers: mediated field experience as a pedagogy for teacher education. *Pedagogies: An International Journal, 10*(2), pp. 149–76.

Lemov, D., 2010. *Teach Like a Champion: 49 Techniques That Put Students on the Path to College (K–12).* New York: John Wiley & Sons.

Marzano, R.J., Marzano, J.S. and Pickering, D., 2003. *Classroom Management that Works: Research-Based Strategies for Every Teacher.* Alexandria, VA: ASCD.

Miao, Z., Reynolds, D., Harris, A. and Jones, M., 2015. Comparing performance: a cross-national investigation into the teaching of mathematics in primary classrooms in England and China. *Asia Pacific Journal of Education, 35*(3), pp. 392–403.

O'Neill, S.C. and Stephenson, J., 2014. Evidence-based classroom and behaviour management content in Australian pre-service primary teachers' coursework: Wherefore art thou? *Australian Journal of Teacher Education (Online), 39*(4), p. 1.

Rosenshine, B., 2012. Principles of instruction: research-based strategies that all teachers should know. *American Educator, 36*(1), p. 12.

Ross, L., 1977. The intuitive psychologist and his shortcomings: distortions in the attribution process. *Advances in Experimental Social Psychology, 10*, pp. 173–220.

Smith, B., 2016. books flat, ruler on line, number lines – cold calling – all ways to keep kids on toes & easier for teacher to check. 21 November. Available from: https://twitter.com/BarryNSmith79/status/800561820079714304.

Tauber, R.T., 1999. *Classroom Management: Sound Theory and Effective Practice.* Chicago, IL: Greenwood Publishing Group.

Wheldall, K., 1991. Managing troublesome classroom behaviour in regular schools: a positive teaching perspective. *International Journal of Disability, Development and Education, 38*(2), pp. 99–116.

Wheldall, K. and Bradd, L., 2013. Classroom seating arrangements and classroom behaviour. *Developments in Educational Psychology*, pp. 181–95.

Wiliam, D., 2011. *Embedded Formative Assessment.* Bloomington, IN: Solution Tree Press.

Wong, C., Odom, S.L., Hume, K.A., Cox, A.W., Fettig, A., Kucharczyk, S., Brock, M.E., Plavnick, J.B., Fleury, V.P. and Schultz, T.R., 2015. Evidence-based practices for children, youth, and young adults with autism spectrum disorder: a comprehensive review. *Journal of Autism and Developmental Disorders, 45*(7), pp. 1951–66.

3

THE SCIENCE OF LEARNING

Key Points

This chapter will:

- Offer a working definition of 'learning'
- Describe how the limitations of the human mind affect how we learn
- Offer strategies for working with, and overcoming, these limitations
- Discuss the differences between things we have evolved to learn and academic learning
- Explain the difference between novices and experts and discuss the problem of transferring learning to new contexts

Academic learning is unnatural

So, what is the difference between learning vocabulary and learning, say, how to multiply fractions or how to read? To many generations of education reformers, there *was* no difference. The fact that school learning was laborious compared to more natural kinds of learning led them to the conclusion that schools were badly designed and teaching was artificial (Egan, 2004).

The psychologist David Geary has developed an interesting theory that might explain why there really is a difference between learning to listen to speech and learning to read. To Geary, listening to speech is 'biologically primary' and reading is 'biologically secondary' (Geary, 1995).

Geary's theory boils down to a simple question: what kinds of learning has evolution had the time to act on? We have been speaking to each other for hundreds of thousands, perhaps millions, of years. This means that the process by which we learn spoken language, including the means by which we learn oral vocabulary, has had the time to be subjected to evolution; we may have evolved a mental module of some kind that is set up specifically to learn this. However, writing was invented only around 3200 BCE (Schmandt-Besserat, 2016). This is relatively recent, and for much of the time since then it has been the preserve of a small elite. We have not had sufficient time for natural selection to act and evolve ways to naturally learn the mechanics of reading and writing.

Geary contends that things that we learn effortlessly, such as speaking or walking, are all the kinds of skills and knowledge that we have evolved to acquire. Schools were created precisely because our modern society accumulates knowledge across generations that *cannot* easily be learnt in this way. Such learning is effortful and incremental. The understandable goal of making academic subjects as natural to learn as learning to speak is a goal that is probably doomed to failure.

Although the specifics of Geary's theory are hard to confirm, it does provide a plausible explanation for the kinds of results we see in cognitive science where academic learning seems to be subject to constraints that natural learning circumvents. It also may explain why the efforts of the early 20th century's progressive educators to make academic learning more natural and spontaneous seem to have largely failed.

What is learning?

In the previous chapter we explored the importance of creating the right conditions for academic, biologically secondary learning to take place. A positive environment is certainly very helpful, but it is not sufficient. We cannot necessarily assume that if students appear to be cooperative and well behaved then they will be learning. In fact, this is something of a trap that teachers can fall into. There are plenty of students whose lack of understanding will be hidden from the teacher because they do not outwardly misbehave or complain (see Stowe et al., 1999, for example).

This is at the heart of many criticisms of traditional forms of education, criticisms that view traditional approaches as ones that prioritise discipline and obedience (Leland and Kasten, 2002). Yes, children may be subdued but this is not the same as helping them progress in their understanding of the world or to think critically about the ideas that are presented to them. It is quite possible to imagine an orderly classroom where students are completing routine or irrelevant tasks from which they gain little, just as it is quite possible to imagine a rowdy classroom where at least some of the children are learning.

Part of a teacher's job is to make selections from different possible classroom activities. Teachers need to consider the classroom management implications of those selections but, primarily, they will seek activities that maximise what their students learn. In order to do this well, it is helpful to have a theory of how learning occurs.

This chapter employs a simple theory of learning based upon a model in which the mind consists of two main parts; a working memory that acts as a bottleneck to new academic concepts, and an effectively limitless long-term memory (Figure 3.1). Moreover, new academic knowledge passing into the long-term memory has to pass through the working memory. These different parts are not meant to correspond to specific regions of the brain and this model is not intended to be comprehensive. From time to time, we will need to add a layer or two. So, think of it more as a 'good-enough' heuristic to use in order to help us make better teaching decisions.

If we want to consider what the process of learning involves then we need to decide what we mean by 'learning'. Kirschner et al. (2006) define learning as a change in long-term memory. This seems like a

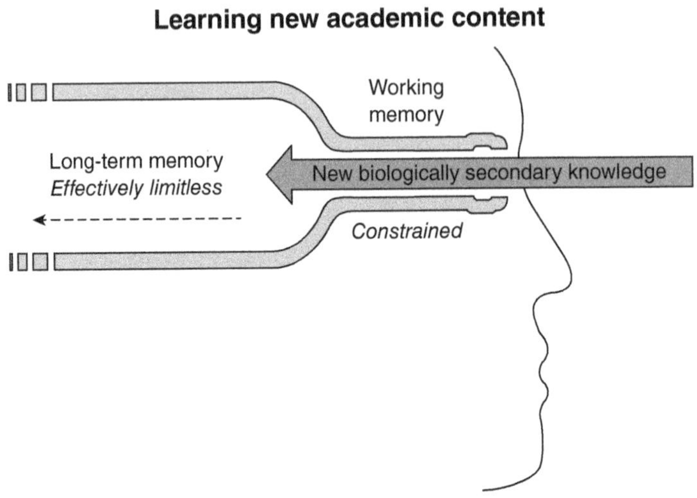

Learning new academic content

Figure 3.1 Working memory is like a bottleneck in the mind when dealing with new, biologically secondary knowledge.

good place to start. If something has not changed in your long-term memory then it is hard to argue that you have learnt anything. And it is clear that we all have long-term memories, whether you are convinced by the rest of the model or not. So, the question of how we create learning is one of how we enable changes to occur, and persist, in long-term memory.

There is another logical consequence of defining learning in this way; we cannot see it. When we test students, ask them questions or require them to demonstrate a skill then we are observing a *behaviour*. This is why it is called 'behavioural research' and it does not mean that we are necessarily researching discipline problems. Whenever we draw inferences from behaviours, whether these involve swearing at a teacher or answering questions on a test, we are inferring cognitive processes from behavioural activity.

In recent years, neuroscience has made great strides in imaging the workings of living brains but it would be fanciful to assume that we will be able to observe changes in specific memories any time soon. Neuroscience deals largely with the flow of blood and differences in electrical potentials. We know that these are *linked* to mental activity but we do not really know how. At the moment, neuroscience offers little to help us understand teaching and learning and it has even been argued that it is unlikely to do so in the future (Bowers, 2016).

The good news is that behavioural research can, and often does, allow us to draw strong conclusions about learning, even if we cannot see it directly. Of all such research, basic cognitive science has the potential to best explain the process of learning, rather than large-scale trials of different teaching methods. It is basic cognitive science that informs the model of the mind in this book.

Overcoming our constraints

Back in 1956, George A. Miller wrote about a key insight in the journey towards a model of learning. His paper 'The magical number seven, plus or minus two: some limits on our capacity for processing information' is now something of a classic. He presented evidence from experiments where test subjects were given a list of numbers or words which they then had to repeat back. The length of the longest list that these subjects could accurately recall is a test of what Miller called 'immediate' memory (immediate memory, working memory and another phrase, 'short-term' memory, are not identical ideas, but they are close enough in meaning for the purposes of this discussion). The number of items that could be recalled varied from an average of nine items for remembering a string of zeros and ones, down to five items for a string of single-syllable words.

Miller also asked an important question: what is an item? The word 'pit' for instance is one syllable but consists of three distinct sounds: 'p', 'i' and 't'. So, what is it that makes this *one* item of information and not *three*? The answer is something quite important to our story. English speakers generally have a concept in their long-term memories of what a 'pit' is. Once we have stored a concept in this way, we can manipulate it as a single item: this process is known as 'chunking'. We also do not have to remember the sequence of different sounds because this is something that we already know.

Imagine I wanted you to remember a string of six digits for the next half-an-hour. Which string would be easier to remember; 'xkwvgt' or 'spider'? It would be easier to remember 'spider' because you have a concept of it in your long-term memory. To remember 'xkwvgt' requires remembering a number of items and their relationship to each other whereas to remember 'spider', we just have to remember the one thing.

From this, we can draw two clear principles: working memory is very limited, but these constraints fall away if we are able to draw upon stuff that we have already stored in our long-term memory. This is transformative, removing the bottleneck and allowing us to manipulate far more information.

Despite the widespread myth that you can learn things by playing audio recordings while sleeping (Simon and Emmons, 1956; Taylor and Kowalski, 2012), there is little evidence to suggest that academic, biologically secondary concepts can pass directly into the long-term memory without passing first through the working memory, and this gives us some clue as to why learning is such a painstaking and cumulative process. When we know little of a field, we have to process discrete bits of information, and so we need to be presented with only a few new concepts at a time. Once we have started to store relevant knowledge in our long-term memory, we can begin to chunk new concepts. Novices cannot gather new knowledge at the same rate as experts in the same area.

Taking a load off

If working memory is so tightly constrained when learning new academic concepts, then it follows that teachers should seek to reduce the strain on it. This idea has been confirmed by John Sweller and colleagues in a series of experiments that demonstrate what has become known as the 'worked-example effect' (Sweller et al., 2011). This effect has been shown across different age-groups and with different subject matter.

In a typical experiment, participants are randomly allocated to one of two groups. The first group is given a series of, for example, algebra problems to solve and the second group is given worked examples of those same problems to study. Both groups are then tested on their ability to solve similar problems. The result is that the group that studied the worked examples performs better on this test.

This contradicts the intuitive idea that we learn more by figuring things out for ourselves than by being told how to do something, and so it is an important result. Moreover, it seems to align with the idea of a constrained working memory: problem solving overloads the capacity of working memory and even if the problems are solved correctly there is little capacity left for learning, i.e. the transfer of these solution strategies into long-term memory.

Yet this finding seems to be at odds with another robust result from cognitive science research, that of the 'generation effect'. In a typical study of this kind, students are again randomly allocated to one of two groups. The first group is given a list of word pairs, such as 'long–short', that consist of a stimulus and a response that are connected by a rule; the rule in this case is that the words are opposites. The second group has to generate the second word from the stimulus word, the first letter of the response and the rule. So, in this case, they would be given, 'long–s'. When later presented with the stimulus words, the group who had to generate their own answers perform better at selecting the correct response than those who were simply given both words.

In the case of the worked-example effect it seems that *reducing* the load on working memory is beneficial whereas with the generation effect it seems that *increasing* the load on working memory is beneficial. How can these results be reconciled?

A clue can be found in an extension of the worked-example effect. If you perform the same experiment with worked examples and problem solving but you give these to domain *experts*, people who already know how to solve algebra problems, for instance, you find that the experts learn more from solving problems than from studying worked examples. The worked-example effect reverses (Kalyuga et al., 2003).

If you think about the difference between solving an algebra problem and remembering a stimulus-response word, then it is apparent that these tasks vary in complexity. To solve an algebra problem, you need to take account of a number of elements, the symbols, whilst also paying attention to the rules that govern their relationships. This can easily overload working memory. The worked examples focus attention on the correct solution pathways and so reduce this load.

In comparison, the word stimulus–response task is very simple. It is quite possible to read pairs of such words without really thinking about them much at all. Although overloading the working memory will not lead to learning, neither will tasks that do not engage working memory. If learning has to pass through the working memory, then it must be active in some way.

So, there is a sweet spot. Very simple tasks need to have a little difficulty added to them so that some active processing takes place whereas more complex tasks need to be broken down, simplified and modelled so as not to overwhelm novices. The fact that experts learn more by solving algebra problems can then be explained by the fact that they already know the solution pathways and so the constraints on working memory fall away. Reading the worked examples is redundant, does not add much value and may even interfere with what the expert already knows. At least by solving problems experts may gain additional practice and learn to apply their understanding to variations of the original problem. The active processing this involves causes the learning.

The path of progress

So far, we have imagined novices and experts as different individuals and yet, if all goes well, our students should gradually progress from one to the other. This seems to imply a learning pathway where complex concepts such as algebra problems should first be taught in ways that minimise cognitive load but as students progress in their learning, they need to spend more time solving variations of the original problem themselves.

The rate at which we can progress from the use of worked examples and equivalent forms of strong guidance to problem solving and generating answers will depend on our students and the complexity of the material. Very simple material, such as the word stimulus–response task, may benefit from generation from the outset. Moderately challenging material that involves remembering key facts or ideas from a given context may require some initial strong guidance, but it will be optimal to quickly move on to testing and generation. More complex material might require extended amounts of gradually fading guidance or repeated exposure to guidance before students benefit from solving problems on their own.

The idea of 'element interactivity' has been proposed as a description of these differences in complexity (Chen et al., 2016a). Some evidence is starting to emerge in support of this idea but, at the time of writing, it is not universally accepted. Individual researchers tend

Table 3.1   Teaching strategies must take into account the expertise of the students and the complexity of the content. *(Based on Chen et al., 2016b.)*

Which is the optimal instructional strategy?	Low element interactivity	High element interactivity
Low expertise	Generation	Worked examples
High expertise	Generation	Generation (i.e.problem solving)

to work either with experiments involving simple tasks or those that involve more complex tasks and therefore they tend to see the issue from one perspective only. Experiments that vary the level of complexity are rare but such experiments are beginning to be conducted (e.g. Chen et al., 2016b).

Once a concept has been learnt, the benefit of generating answers is not limited to simply engaging the working memory and this brings us on to the next important point. We have defined learning as a change in long-term memory but how long is 'long term'? Many teachers will have had the experience of a student who remembers something a week after it was taught but who seems to have totally forgotten it after a few months. Both memories are technically 'long term' and this exposes a weakness in our simple model because remembering something for just a few weeks seems educationally useless.

We should not despair. Even if students do appear to have forgotten something then there is strong evidence that they will learn it more quickly the next time that they are exposed to the concept (Willingham, 2015). And there is plenty that we can do to help memories persist.

It seems that the mind does not store memories as if they are in some sort of filing cabinet. Instead, there is a process whereby memories that are accessed more frequently become easier to retrieve. This is the basis of an important phenomenon known as the 'testing effect' or the effect of 'retrieval practice' (Karpicke, 2012). There are two names for the same idea because 'testing' has gathered negative connotations in recent years. We will look in more detail at how to make use of effects like the testing effect in the chapter on planning lessons.

We need to be clear that there is a difference between marching students into an exam hall to sit a standardised test and asking them a few recall questions at the start of a class. The latter is about disrupting the process of forgetting. It trains students' brains that this particular knowledge is going to continue to be important over time and so is not something that should be left to wither and die. It also helps students associate the right cues with the right knowledge; they learn what to retrieve in response to a particular question.

We must also remember that the answers students give, the behaviour, is not the same thing as their learning. Students may answer incorrectly and require feedback. They may experience this process as an uncomfortable one because they may have been under the impression that they had learnt the concept better than this test seems to demonstrate. Nevertheless, quizzing will generally improve the later retrieval strength of the correct concepts provided that incorrect responses are corrected by the teacher (Roediger and Butler, 2011). It is worth expanding a little on the issue of cues and how retrieval helps.

Transferring learning to new contexts

There is a great deal of research on the differences between novices and experts. Sometimes, this can be used in unhelpful ways. If you are looking for a shortcut then it is tempting to analyse what an expert does and suggest to a novice to 'do that.' Yet experts become experts through extended processes of deliberate practice. You wouldn't put a novice aviator in the cockpit of a passenger jet and ask them to have a go at flying it. There is a lot of learning that would need to take place first, some of which might indeed look a little like flying a plane, but some might look completely different, such as studying for theory examinations.

Still, expert-novice differences can be instructive. We have already seen how experts and novices differ in terms of the worked-example effect. But we can use some clever cognitive research to also draw a few inferences about the different ways in which knowledge is structured in their minds.

In one classic experiment, novice undergraduate physics students were compared with more expert graduate students (Chi et al., 1981). They were given a set of physics problems and asked to classify them into categories of their choice. The novices tended to choose categories that related to concrete features of the questions. For instance, they might place all the problems involving an object on a slope into the same category. The experts classified the problems in terms of the physics *principles* required in order to solve the problem.

This demonstrates the way that novices tend to focus on the surface features of problems whereas experts focus on the deep structure (Willingham, 2002). Novices associate a particular kind of response or solution with a particular context whereas experts can see beyond the context to the underlying principles. Through repeated retrieval practice, we can cycle students through a range of contexts so that they eventually come to give responses that relate to the concepts and principles rather than being distracted by the specifics.

So experts do not simply have more knowledge than novices, it is organised in more productive ways.

This is key to one of the thorniest problems in education: transfer. It is very hard for students to transfer what they have learnt to new situations. A number of teaching approaches have been proposed that are intended to promote transfer and so it is worth reviewing these.

There are also those who advocate for project-based or inquiry models where learning is situated within realistic contexts. The rationale is that this will encourage students to apply their learning more widely. Yet it is unclear why students would not be distracted by the surface features of a real-world context any more than they would by a more standard classroom approach. There is some evidence to back these techniques, although it appears to be fairly limited (see Hmelo-Silver et al., 2007, for example).

The most stunning experimental results in support of a particular teaching method leading to transfer probably come from the Cognitive Acceleration in Science Education (CASE) research of the early 1990s. Over the course of two years, one science lesson every two weeks was replaced with lessons based upon principles outlined by Piaget and Vygotsky. Students were required to work in groups and solve tricky scientific problems. When tracked up to five years later, these students showed gains in their scores on an *English* exam, when compared to a control group (Adey and Shayer, 1993).

These are extraordinary results because transfer of this kind is exceptionally rare. In 2013 the Education Endowment Foundation in England attempted to replicate these findings with a randomised controlled trial of a slightly scaled-back version of CASE known as 'Let's Think Secondary Science'. Unfortunately, they did not find the same results. The students involved in the programme actually performed worse than the control group on later English and maths assessments, although this result could have arisen by chance (Hanley et al., 2016).

The objective of transfer seems more achievable if we can identify general cognitive capacities or thinking skills that we can apply in a range of situations. A good analogy here is a muscle – you train it, it grows bigger and then you can use it in a range of different ways. Like the brain, we have evolved muscles but we can also change the capabilities of muscles through exercise. Perhaps we can train the brain.

There are a number of ways that we might attempt to do this. A popular idea at present is to give people computer games to play with the express purpose of improving some cognitive capacity. Unfortunately, studies seem to indicate that whilst people improve at playing the game, this does not transfer to other tasks (Simons et al., 2016).

A less fundamental approach might involve training people to apply heuristics or, as Carl Bereiter describes them, 'step-wise procedures' to the way that they think through problems and tasks (Bereiter, 2005). These are often described as 'critical thinking skills'. However, as Bereiter notes, the heuristics that people tend to compose often do not represent the *actual* processes of thinking that are revealed when we ask people to think aloud. It seems that we impose order, after the fact, on the way that we think.

Nonetheless, there is evidence that some of these heuristics can improve performance. Particularly encouraging is research into reading comprehension strategies. As an example of such a strategy, a student might be asked to generate her own questions while reading a text (Willingham, 2006). But describing these as cognitive 'skills' seems to be a little flawed because you achieve most of the gains from very brief training and further practice seems to have little effect.

The reason why further training in comprehension skills appears to be redundant is the same reason why thinking skills more generally have a limited impact on our ability to perform tasks and solve problems: they don't get us very far without relevant domain knowledge.

Consider training students to use a general thinking routine for analysing sources and then asking them to apply this to a 1940 American newspaper article about the war in Europe. The students may ask themselves the purpose of the source but if they know little about America's stance at this time or the position of the newspaper then they will struggle to answer these questions. On the other hand, if they *do* possess this knowledge then such a question will be relatively quick and easy to answer. The value of learning the critical thinking routine may be that it acts to prompt students that this is an important aspect to consider when constructing their responses rather than in training them to think in a better way.

Courses in critical thinking may also deal with logical fallacies and knowledge of such fallacies can be extremely powerful in enabling us to identify flawed arguments. But does this constitute a skill? Have we improved thinking? In a way, I suppose that we have, but only in the same way that knowledge of the theory of evolution improves thinking about biology.

A recent review examined the way that attending university affects students' critical thinking and it was overwhelmingly positive (Huber and Kuncel, 2015). It seems that studying at degree-level can lead to large gains in the ability to analyse, ask probing questions and formulate conclusions. Interestingly, the gains were similar for students who studied specific critical thinking units and for those who simply studied traditional subjects, implying that the critical thinking courses added little additional benefit. Perhaps it is the acquisition of powerful knowledge, such as knowledge of evolution, that most enables us to think critically rather than the rehearsal of any specific routines. Indeed, the authors cast doubt on the transferability of critical thinking although they do suggest that one component may stay with us as we move from subject to subject: a general propensity to ask questions and challenge ideas. This is a disposition that we might be able to encourage with the right kind of teaching.

Research into experts and novices may again help us to understand the cognitive processes that are at work when we think like an expert. In 1973, Chase and Simon replicated an earlier set of studies by Adriaan de Groot. De Groot had asked chess players of varying expertise to study a chess board for five seconds. The pieces on the board were arranged as they would have been in the middle of a genuine game. He then asked them to reproduce the pattern of pieces. De Groot found that experts were better at this task than novices.

Chase and Simon added an important variation. They also tested both groups with board arrangements that were random and that could not therefore have come from genuine games of chess.

They found that experts and novices performed at about the same level with the random arrangements; the experts had lost their advantage.

This strongly suggests that the expert chess players had not developed a general-purpose improvement in spatial memory. Instead, their expertise seemed to be closely linked to their knowledge and experience; this expertise would not be likely to transfer out of the area of chess.

The idea that the mind does not consist of general mental muscles that can be applied to many different situations is not new. At the start of the 20th century, the psychologist Edward Thorndike demonstrated that the study of Latin did not improve students' performance in the other subjects that they studied (Perkins and Salomon, 1992). At that time, many people believed that Latin disciplined the mind and that this would have a general benefit.

So, there are few general-purpose shortcuts that enable us to transfer learning rapidly from one situation to another. The most promising strategies seem to be extended periods of academic instruction where students are systematically exposed to a range of different contexts, perhaps with comparisons made between these contexts, and the acquisition of powerful forms of knowledge that can be applied to a range of different situations.

Crystallised intelligence

To understand the way that powerful knowledge may help, it is worth considering a current theory of intelligence. Psychologists have noted that performances on diverse tests of innate ability tend to correlate with each other for any particular individual; if they are proficient on one test then they will tend to be proficient on them all. This overall intelligence seems to be composed of two main components: fluid intelligence and crystallised intelligence (Ellingsen et al., 2016).

Fluid intelligence is essentially our raw processing power and it relates to working memory capacity. Despite the claims made about brain-training, we don't seem to be able to do much about it.

Crystallised intelligence is different. This is the amount of general knowledge that we possess. The good news is that this is highly susceptible to training and it correlates strongly with performance on intelligence-based tasks (Moehring et al., 2016). To understand why, consider being confronted with the task of fixing a kettle: you might try using your fluid intelligence to figure it all out from scratch or you might alternatively rely on crystallised intelligence: perhaps you have fixed a similar kettle before or you have read about how to do it in a book. Similarly, if your car breaks down, who would you hire to fix it? Would you hire someone who has done a course in car repair or someone who has done a course in thinking?

Conclusion

Which returns us neatly to our definition of learning as a change in long-term memory. Change it in productive ways and we grow our students' crystallised intelligence. Pick particularly powerful knowledge, such as the theory of evolution or knowledge of logical fallacies, and we grow this intelligence in ways that can be applied to many situations. These seem like worthwhile goals for teachers; goals that are consistent with the science of learning.

References

Adey, P. and Shayer, M., 1993. An exploration of long-term far-transfer effects following an extended intervention program in the high school science curriculum. *Cognition and instruction, 11*(1), pp. 1–29.

Bereiter, C., 2005. 10 critical thinking, creativity, and other virtues. In *Education and Mind in the Knowledge Age*. Abingdon: Routledge. pp. 356–97.

Bowers, J.S., 2016. The practical and principled problems with educational neuroscience. *Psychological Review, 123*(5), pp. 600–12.

Chase, W.G. and Simon, H.A. (1973) 'Perception in chess'. *Cognitive Psychology, 4*(1), 55–81.

Chen, O., Kalyuga, S. and Sweller, J., 2016a. The expertise reversal effect is a variant of the more general element interactivity effect. *Educational Psychology Review*, pp. 1–13.

Chen, O., Kalyuga, S. and Sweller, J., 2016b. Relations between the worked example and generation effects on immediate and delayed tests. *Learning and Instruction, 45*, pp. 20–30.

Chi, M.T., Feltovich, P.J. and Glaser, R., 1981. Categorization and representation of physics problems by experts and novices. *Cognitive Science, 5*(2), pp. 121–52.

Egan, K., 2004. *Getting It Wrong from the Beginning: Our Progressivist Inheritance from Herbert Spencer, John Dewey, and Jean Piaget*. New Haven, CT: Yale University Press.

Ellingsen, V.J. and Ackerman, P.L., 2016. Fluid–crystallized theory of intelligence. In *The Encyclopedia of Adulthood and Aging*. Hoboken, NJ: Wiley–Blackwell.

Geary, D.C., 1995. Reflections of evolution and culture in children's cognition: implications for mathematical development and instruction. *American Psychologist*, 50(1), p. 24.

Hanley, P., Böhnke, J.R., Slavin, R., Elliott, L. and Croudace, T., 2016. Let's Think Secondary Science: Evaluation report and executive summary. Available at: https://educationendowmentfoundation.org.uk/public/files/Projects/EEF_Project_Report_Lets_Think_Secondary_Science.pdf.

Hmelo-Silver, C.E., Duncan, R.G. and Chinn, C.A., 2007. Scaffolding and achievement in problem-based and inquiry learning: a response to Kirschner, Sweller, and Clark (2006). *Educational Psychologist*, 42(2), pp. 99–107.

Huber, C.R. and Kuncel, N.R., 2015. Does college teach critical thinking? A meta-analysis. *Review of Educational Research*, 86(2), pp.431–468.

Kalyuga, S., Ayres, P., Chandler, P. and Sweller, J., 2003. The expertise reversal effect. *Educational Psychologist*, 38(1), pp. 23–31.

Karpicke, J.D., 2012. Retrieval-based learning active retrieval promotes meaningful learning. *Current Directions in Psychological Science*, 21(3), pp. 157–63.

Kirschner, P.A., Sweller, J. and Clark, R.E., 2006. Why minimal guidance during instruction does not work: an analysis of the failure of constructivist, discovery, problem-based, experiential, and inquiry-based teaching. *Educational Psychologist*, 41(2), pp. 75–86.

Leland, C.H. and Kasten, W.C., 2002. Literacy education for the 21st century: it's time to close the factory. *Reading & Writing Quarterly*, 18(1), pp. 5–15.

Miller, G.A., 1956. The magical number seven, plus or minus two: some limits on our capacity for processing information. *Psychological Review*, 63(2), p. 81.

Moehring, A., Schroeders, U., Leichtmann, B. and Wilhelm, O., 2016. Ecological momentary assessment of digital literacy: influence of fluid and crystallized intelligence, domain-specific knowledge, and computer usage. *Intelligence*, 59, pp.170–180.

Perkins, D.N. and Salomon, G., 1992. Transfer of learning. In *International Encyclopedia of Education*, 2, pp. 6452–7.

Roediger, H.L. and Butler, A.C., 2011. The critical role of retrieval practice in long-term retention. *Trends in Cognitive Sciences*, 15(1), pp. 20–7.

Schmandt-Besserat, D., 2016. *The Evolution of Writing*. [online] Available at: https://sites.utexas.edu/dsb/tokens/the-evolution-of-writing/.

Simon, C.W. and Emmons, W.H., 1956. EEG, consciousness, and sleep. *Science*, 124(3231), pp. 1066–9.

Simons, D.J., Boot, W.R., Charness, N., Gathercole, S.E., Chabris, C.F., Hambrick, D.Z. and Stine-Morrow, E.A., 2016. Do 'brain-training' programs work? *Psychological Science in the Public Interest*, 17(3), pp. 103–86.

Stowe, R.M., Arnold, D.H. and Ortiz, C., 1999. Gender differences in the relationship of language development to disruptive behavior and peer relationships in preschoolers. *Journal of Applied Developmental Psychology*, 20(4), pp. 521–36.

Sweller, J., Ayres, P. and Kalyuga, S., 2011. The worked example and problem completion effects. In *Cognitive Load Theory*. New York: Springer. pp. 99–109.

Taylor, A.K. and Kowalski, P., 2012. Students' misconceptions in psychology: how you ask matters ... sometimes. *Journal of the Scholarship of Teaching and Learning*, 12(3), pp. 62–77.

Willingham, D.T., 2002. Ask the cognitive scientist inflexible knowledge: the first step to expertise. *American Educator*, 26(4), pp. 31–3.

Willingham, D.T., 2006. The usefulness of brief instruction in reading comprehension strategies. *American Educator*, 30(4), pp. 39–45.

Willingham, D.T., 2015. Ask the cognitive scientist: Do students remember what they learn in school? *American Educator*, 39(3), p. 33–8.

4
MOTIVATING STUDENTS

Key Points

This chapter will:

- Outline some different ways of thinking about motivation
- Provide strategies for increasing the motivation and academic engagement of students
- Discuss how some common folk-theories of motivation might lead us into making choices that harm the achievement of students

Why we do the things we do

Human motivations are many and various; noble and selfish. They have inspired great works of art and literature and they have provoked contemplation of the divine. We cannot boldly claim that certain teacher actions will definitely increase motivation. It's too complex. The best we can hope for is to play the odds; create favourable conditions. Fortunately, there are some clues as to how we might do this.

Many people have a folk theory of motivation that goes something like this: make lessons fun and interesting and students will become motivated about the subject and achieve. This approach relies on *situational interest*: 'temporary interest that arises spontaneously due to environmental factors such as task instructions or an engaging text' (Schraw et al., 2001). But isn't there a risk here? What happens when we take the situational interest away? Presumably, a motivated student is one who can persist through the drudgery because he or she is working towards a higher goal. If we train students to expect entertainment, then are we preparing them for this?

It may be common sense to suggest that providing situational interest will lead to better achievement and it explains why motivation and achievement often seem to go hand-in-hand. Yet this is a chicken-and-egg situation. Could it be that achievement causes motivation? Perhaps it is a virtuous circle? And what does a motivated person look like? Perhaps you imagine someone who is busy doing something, smiling and active. And yet we can be motivated to read a book. When I read a book, I sit quite still with a frown on my face. So this is what motivation *can* look like.

We are in a similar situation to one we found ourselves in with learning. We cannot observe learning directly; we have to infer it from performance. And we cannot observe motivation directly either. We can ask students about their level of motivation and this will provide some useful data but we also have to bear in mind that people don't always tell the truth.

We need to constrain our thinking about motivation. It is an obvious point, but we should seek to motivate students about the thing that we want them to learn and not about something else. For instance, imagine a maths class where we ask students to play a card game. They may find the game highly enjoyable but what if it doesn't actually require them to think about much maths? Similarly, students might enjoy making a poster in history class or a diorama in English, yet if these do not require them to think much about academic content then we haven't done anything to motivate them about that content. The lesson a student might learn is that, 'I enjoy the bits of history where we don't do any history'.

In his book *Why Don't Students Like School?* Dan Willingham gives an excellent example of such an activity (Willingham, 2009). The Underground Railroad was a network that helped former slaves escape from the Southern States of the United States prior to the abolition of slavery. A teacher thought it would be a good idea to ask his students to bake the biscuits that were a staple food of the runaway slaves. This might have been a lot of fun but students would have been thinking about flour, mixing the ingredients, cooking the biscuits, and not about the Underground Railroad.

It is with this filter firmly in place that we should consider ways of increasing situational interest. Schraw et al. (2001) have six principles to consider when selecting texts to use in class which might have broader application: offer meaningful choices to students; use well-organised texts; select texts that are vivid perhaps due to the use of suspense or provocation; use texts that students know about; encourage students to be active learners by predicting or summarising; and provide relevance cues to highlight themes or aspects of the text that are relevant to learning.

Let's examine the first suggestion. It is clear that we could offer students choices in ways that might increase situational interest but at the same time redirect attention away from the target academic concepts. The ability to choose a key component of self-determination theory (Ryan and Deci, 2000) and the view that a certain level of autonomy is motivating. Unfortunately, relative novices in a particular field are not well-placed to make good choices about what and how to learn (Kirschner and van Merriënboer, 2013). To put it plainly: they don't know what they don't know.

A series of experiments reviews by Richard Clark in the early 1980s illustrate this point well (Clark, 1982). Students were offered a choice of activity. Low ability students tended to prefer more open activities whereas higher ability students preferred more structured activities. And yet these choices were the opposite of those that would have maximised learning. One possible explanation is that students choose a method that they perceive will require the least effort; they therefore invest less effort and so achieve less (Robinson and Bligh, 2016).

It therefore seems wise to tightly constrain any choices that we offer students. As a young science teacher, I would sometimes ask my students to design a poster about a topic that we were studying. After half-an-hour, I would notice that some students had spent the time meticulously crafting a title and that others had beautifully drawn a single picture. I soon learnt to specify certain content and give time-limits for producing particular aspects of the poster, which I would then actively monitor.

Self-determination theory is concerned with fostering *intrinsic* motivation, motivation that comes from within, rather than motivating individuals through the use of carrots and sticks. This is highly desirable and something that teachers will want to promote. Besides autonomy, two more needs are suggested by the theory: the need for competence and the need for relatedness.

Relatedness is, 'the need to feel belongingness and connectedness with others' (Ryan and Deci, 2000) and is clearly affected by school and classroom culture. This is why positive teacher–student relationships built on mutual respect are associated with improved academic outcomes (Roorda et al., 2011). It is pretty hard to achieve such relationships in a context of poor classroom management.

Relatedness has even been tested experimentally. In an intriguing randomised controlled trial conducted by American researchers, teachers and students were given information about what they had in common (Gehlbach et al., 2016). This then seemed to positively impact on the course grades awarded by the teachers, perhaps due to either improved academic performance or teacher perceptions. Teachers' feelings of relatedness towards their students also seem to correlate with their happiness in the job, even more so than relatedness to colleagues (Klassen et al., 2012).

The feeling of competence is the third need identified by self-determination theory and it is interesting to note that it is this need that impacts upon our chicken-and-egg question. Psychologists have created two slightly different ways of describing competence: 'self-concept' is a general feeling of competence within a particular field and 'self-efficacy' is the belief that you can complete a specific task.

It is the difference between thinking you are a good writer and thinking that you are capable of writing a decent report for your boss.

If feelings of competence improve levels of motivation, then we would expect achievement to improve future motivation by enhancing feelings of competence. If this is the case, we need to look for teaching activities that lead to academic achievement and this is a convenient result because it removes some potential for conflict between prioritising motivation and prioritising achievement.

Such a proposal is supported by evidence from a longitudinal Canadian study of primary school maths (Garon-Carrier et al., 2016). Researchers followed students from Grade 1 through to Grade 4, at each point giving them a survey to find their intrinsic motivation towards maths and recording their scores in maths assessment. Motivation in earlier grades did not predict performance in later grades. In other words, more motivated Grade 1 students did not tend to be better at maths in Grade 2. However, achievement *did* predict later motivation. So, for example, students who achieved well in Grade 2 were more likely to feel motivated about maths in Grade 4 (see Figure 4.1).

This study suggests a one-way relationship between achievement and motivation, with the former causing the latter. If confirmed, it would imply that attempts to motivate students are quite misguided; we should simply focus on achievement. However, this is just one study, in one subject and age-group, so we should not extrapolate too eagerly and I cannot imagine many teachers seeking to choose a dull and dreary approach if they can think of a different one that will generate more situational interest. Other studies suggest that the relationship between motivation and achievement is

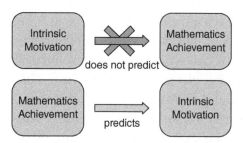

Figure 4.1   The relationship between intrinsic motivation and mathematics achievement (*Based on: Garon-Carrier et al., 2016*)

two-way (e.g. Putwain et al., 2017), and this would seem to be a more intuitive finding.

A seemingly paradoxical relationship can be drawn from data collected in international tests (Loveless, 2015). This found a negative relationship between the 2012 Programme for International Student Assessment (PISA) maths scores and measures of motivation – the higher the motivation, the worse the scores. More importantly, when individual countries increase levels of intrinsic motivation over time these scores fall, but when they reduce motivation, they rise.

This seemingly contradicts the usual association between achievement and motivation. However, it can be explained if increased motivation typically comes from increases in situational interest that do not directly lead to greater maths achievement, such as in the card game activity I mentioned above. These activities would crowd out space for other tasks that are more likely to lead to mathematics proficiency; a worrying idea given the tendency for commentators and policymakers to suggest that the route to improved performance in science and mathematics is to make these subjects more enjoyable at school.

Stories as a lever for learning

It is worth returning to Schraw et al.'s (2001) list of strategies that promote situational interest in a text and examining some of these in more detail because they relate to themes and tensions.

Stories seems to be 'psychologically privileged' by the human mind (Willingham, 2009). The idea of making them 'vivid' will probably increase not only situational interest but also memory. As long as this is a memory that we want the students to retain then we have a happy confluence of aims. Again, it is worth injecting a note of caution. An exploding hydrogen balloon is likely to be so vivid that students won't recall the explanation given at the same time. This shouldn't lead us to abandon such demonstrations but we cannot assume that they will lead to powerful learning unless the ideas are revisited at a later point.

The typical arc of a story consists of an introduction to the setting and characters, a problem or conflict that needs to be solved, further complications added to the solving of that problem and then a resolution. You can follow this narrative arc whether you are telling a fictional story or not. You can even use this structure as a format for a lesson plan. As ever, the key is to ensure that the problems and conflicts align with the ones that you want your students to think about.

This is often where game-based learning falls down. Computer games seem to offer great potential for learning. In particular, they are able to motivate players to engage for extended periods of time whilst solving complex problems. Often, these are individuals who are turned-off by school-based education. It would be great if we could leverage computer games to deliver this kind of engagement in the classroom.

The difficulty arises from the kinds of narrative elements that make computer games addictive. These are not usually the kinds of items that we want students to think about in an educational context. Think of a typical platform game where a character has to collect tokens whilst avoiding the bad guys. How could you leverage that kind of game-play to teach something like history? What historical skill or knowledge could that match? The closest parallel that I can picture between a game and a desired learning objective is between simulations and physical skills: a driving game, for instance, could plausibly act to improve some aspect of real-world driving skills.

Due to the mismatch, many educational games miss the target and have a bolt-on narrative or gameplay aspect that does not relate to the intended learning. Consider again the platform game: we might require students to answer a history question in order to claim the token. Yet this makes the game-play itself semantically irrelevant. It is therefore not surprising that some studies have shown educational games to lead to similar or worse learning outcomes than simply presenting a slide show of the relevant content (see Adams et al., 2012 for example). In a paper sceptical about the claims made for game-based learning, John L. Sherry (2013) compares the 'scientific' approach used in the development of the educational television show *Sesame Street*, to our current understanding of educational computer games, finds the latter wanting and lists a series of research questions that still need to be answered before we can hope to use games as an effective learning tool.

Nevertheless, properly designed, we should be able to use computer games to at least take advantage of the testing effect that we met in Chapter 3. This would mean reducing extraneous gameplay to a minimum so that students spend most of their time thinking about the target content. An example of a game that might fit this profile is

Fling the Teacher, written by Andrew Field and popular in many classrooms. It is a cross between *Hangman* and *Who Wants to be a Millionaire?*. Players must correctly answer a sequence of multiple choice questions in order to construct a catapult and fling a cartoon teacher through the air. Teachers are able to upload their own questions and the program will randomly select from them. This kind of game could help increase situational interest in the otherwise dull activity of answering revision questions.

Authentic or mundane?

When Schraw et al. (2001) suggest that we select texts that students know about, this can send us in one of two directions, as they acknowledge. The first is to try to use contexts for learning that are familiar to students, an idea that is often described in terms of 'relevance' or 'authenticity' and that has social and political overtones. The second approach is to provide students with unfamiliar contexts but teach them about those contexts in advance.

It is easy to see why an unfamiliar context may be demotivating. You need to understand over 90% of the vocabulary used in a text in order to be able to properly comprehend it (Hirsch, 2003) and it seems reasonable to assume that you also need the same level of semantic knowledge – an understanding of the ideas and concepts that are being addressed. There is nothing motivating about incomprehension.

If we make contexts relevant so that they are the kinds of contexts that students are familiar with then we can aid the process of comprehension. This is a larger idea than simply ensuring that students have background knowledge. Relevance may enable students to see the practical applications of an abstract idea (Assor et al., 2002) and it may make students feel included who might otherwise feel alienated if required to work with contexts that are unfamiliar or characteristic of a different, perhaps more privileged group within society (Hastie et al., 2006).

Unfortunately, relevance, or 'authenticity', is something of a unicorn. The answer to the question 'When will I ever need this?' is mostly, 'You won't'. We can survive the modern world with very little education. You can go to the supermarket and buy food without doing any mental arithmetic, should you choose. Knowledge does not generally act as a key that opens doors that would otherwise be inaccessible. It is not binary in that way. Instead, it is more like a continuum; increased levels of knowledge generally increase quality of life (Ceci and Williams, 1997). But you could easily point to any *one* thing and make a strong case that it is quite possible to exist without knowing about it.

When people try to define a relevant curriculum they therefore struggle and draw seemingly perverse conclusions. In his recent book *Future Wise* (Perkins, 2014), David Perkins steered-clear of a strictly functional view of education, aware of the contradictions. Instead, he attempted to define what he termed a 'lifeworthy' curriculum consisting of elements that are 'likely to matter in the lives learners are likely to live'. The end result, where knowledge of the French Revolution is included but quadratic equations are not, seems to speak more to an individual's particular tastes than a coherent selection principle.

At one point, we are advised that a good activity might be one where 'students plan for their town's future water needs or model its traffic flow'. This does not strike me as particularly motivating, no matter how relevant it may be. Instead, it seems quite mundane and boring. At this stage we might wonder whether we have passed right through the motivational effects of relevance and out the other side.

The alternative way of ensuring that students have the right background knowledge – teach the knowledge in advance – may ultimately be more productive. It also provides us with a planning insight; relatively complex tasks set in unfamiliar contexts should not be placed at the start of a teaching sequence.

The teaching of background knowledge can be achieved in both broad and more specific ways. Specifically, we might decide at the outset of a project on trees to spend a few lessons teaching students the names and ideas that are likely to be relevant. A much more difficult task might be to try to generally teach background knowledge that will help you in many different areas.

Core knowledge

The Core Knowledge curriculum developed by E.D. Hirsch's Core Knowledge Foundation attempts to equip elementary school students with the kind of general knowledge that they would need to engage with common texts, an example of which might be a report in a quality newspaper (Hirsch, 2006). Hirsch's curriculum has come in for some criticism. Despite his professed left-wing political leanings (Tyre, 2014), he has been described as a 'neoconservative' whose position on schooling, 'is founded on a sort of cultural supremacy that fails to recognize itself as such' (Buras, 1999).

Hirsch favours the building of broad general knowledge as an approach to reading comprehension rather than the popular practice of teaching reading comprehension 'skills' such as learning to make inferences. If we label something as a 'skill' then this implies that we can improve at it through practice. However, the effects of teaching such reading strategies, although providing an initial boost to reading ability, wash-out fairly quickly with repeated practice adding little extra value (Willingham, 2006).

Hirsch's explanation for the failure of reading comprehension strategies is fairly easy to illustrate. For instance, the following is an extract from the abstract of an academic paper about statistical methods (Rubin, 1978):

> Causal effects are comparisons among values that would have been observed under all possible assignments of treatments to experimental units. In an experiment, one assignment of treatments is chosen and only the values under that assignment can be observed. Bayesian inference for causal effects follows from finding the predictive distribution of the values under the other assignments of treatments. This perspective makes clear the role of mechanisms that sample experimental units, assign treatments and record data.

If you are an educated adult with no background in statistics then it is likely that you were able to read all of the words and still not understand the passage. Applying common reading comprehension strategies is unlikely to be helpful. For instance, monitoring your own comprehension of the passage as you read it is likely to lead to confirmation that you don't understand it. Asking yourself questions as you read the passage – What is the author's purpose? – will likely not bear fruit because you won't be able to answer those questions.

This is the position that many struggling young readers find themselves in when reading passages that are relatively simple for educated adults to comprehend. This is because educated adults possess a lot of knowledge of the world, the extent of which it is easy to underestimate. Hirsch's argument is that we should try to teach that knowledge rather than spend quite as much time practising reading comprehension routines.

There is little large-scale experimental evidence to show that a core knowledge curriculum leads to greater reading comprehension. Experiments of this kind would be costly due to their necessarily long-term nature. Instead, the argument rests on cognitive science and, to a lesser extent, correlational studies that show that academic achievement tends to fall when countries move away from a curriculum that rigorously specifies the knowledge that is to be taught to children (Hirsch, 2016).

The counterargument to Hirsch cuts across motivational and moral lines. Who decides what to include in a core knowledge curriculum? If we use culture *as it is* as our guide then the works of dead white males might predominate. Perhaps we should engineer the curriculum to be a little more socially just than that?

And how will such a curriculum be relevant to the lives of children in inner cities or from ethnic minorities? How will it respect indigenous cultures?

The antithesis of a core knowledge curriculum is probably the 'expanding horizons' social studies curriculum that has been popular in the United States for much of the 20th century and that forms a basis for the Humanities and Social Sciences section of the current Australian Curriculum (ACARA, 2015).

The idea behind 'expanding horizons' is that the curriculum should start with the child and gradually work its way outwards. Typically, children will first investigate their own family relationships then their community and so on. It is only later that they are deemed ready to investigate times and places at a significant remove from their own.

The rationale is again to engage children through relevance and authenticity and yet the 'expanding horizons' model has been criticised for making Social Studies a deeply unpopular course in American schools. The critic Kieran Egan makes the important point that children are fascinated by stories of monsters, witches, wizards and far-off times and places. It is simply not motivationally necessary to start with the child and work your way out (Egan, 1980).

Of course, where learning objectives do *naturally* align with concepts or activities in a student's life then it would be an oversight not to point this out. For instance, a discussion of the abstract concepts of static electricity should include references to the kinds of situations that students might experience where they put on a sweater and their hair stands on end.

Hands-on

Another seemingly obvious idea is that practical work is motivating. As a science teacher, I have no doubt that, to an extent, this is true. Although this motivational effect may not be uniform, with some students preferring more cerebral pursuits.

In a fascinating article for *Quillette* magazine, philosopher and write Emma C. Williams (2016) describes how she was turned off science for life by 'humdrum' experiments where a powder changed from one colour into another. As an adult, she realises that science has the ability to address the deep philosophical questions that she was interested in at the time and remains interested in to this day. Yet she never realised this whilst absently spooning salts into test-tubes in her school science lab.

More fundamentally, we must again ensure that any motivational use of practical work does not motivate students about something *other* than the content that we wish to teach. It is this effect that may be behind an interesting finding from the 2015 round of PISA where students who reported completing the most practical work in science lessons achieved less well in science (OECD, 2016).

This result could be because the practical work displaced the learning of science or it could be because teachers are using practical work in an attempt to motivate lower achieving students. This does not mean that practical work cannot be used well in the teaching of a subject like science. Instead, it suggests that it is not a magic bullet; a finding that should be unsurprising to seasoned observers of education's cycles and fancies.

Minds-on

There is one remaining suggestion from Schraw et al. (2001) that we have not yet addressed and that is the idea of asking students to make predictions and to summarise when reading texts. The broader principle at play here is often known as 'active learning'.

Broadly speaking, it is a good idea to require students to interact with content, particularly if there is a chance that they may drift away from attending to the lesson. It is likely that situational interest causes students to become more active learners – these are the students who might spontaneously take notes during a lecture – but perhaps this also works the other way around. For instance, one finding from the research on worked examples is that students who were required to complete a problem after studying a worked example were likely to pay more attention to the worked example (Sweller et al., 2011). We may not think of this as building long-term intrinsic motivation but it does provide a short-term, extrinsic reason to pay attention to what is being taught.

The bulk of the evidence for active learning comes from studies in higher education. There are many examples of such experiments but, typically, a straight, non-interactive lecture is compared to a condition that requires students to do something with the information that is being conveyed. For instance, one active learning condition might involve issuing students with voting buttons so that they can answer multiple choice questions posed by the lecturer. Another condition might involve the use of worksheets or group discussion. The evidence for active learning that emerges from these studies is relatively strong in terms of both the effect on students' test scores and drop-out rates (Freeman et al., 2014).

These findings from higher education are further bolstered by evidence from process–product studies of school classrooms where 'academic learning time' was found to be a feature of the most effective classrooms (Yates, 2005).

Conclusion

We must be wary of folk theories of motivation. In particular, we need to be careful not to motivate students by something other than the content we are trying to teach. Happily, the goal of maximising our students' achievement may align well with the goal of promoting long-term intrinsic motivation. Yet individuals are complex; a practical activity that science teachers think is really exciting could be humdrum for some of their students.

We should certainly emphasise the relevance of academic content to everyday life but this probably does not need to drive our selection of academic content in the first place. Many children love fairy stories but I have yet to meet one that has a real-life Tinkerbell at home.

References

Adams, D.M., Mayer, R.E., MacNamara, A., Koenig, A. and Wainess, R., 2012. Narrative games for learning: testing the discovery and narrative hypotheses. *Journal of Educational Psychology*, *104*(1), p. 235.

Assor, A., Kaplan, H. and Roth, G., 2002. Choice is good, but relevance is excellent: autonomy-enhancing and suppressing teacher behaviours predicting students' engagement in schoolwork. *British Journal of Educational Psychology*, *72*(2), pp. 261–78.

Australian Curriculum and Assessment Reporting Authority (ACARA), 2015. *Foundation to Year 10 Curriculum: Humanities and Social Sciences*. Retrieved from www.australiancurriculum.edu.au/humanities-and-social-sciences/.

Buras, K.L., 1999. Questioning core assumptions: a critical reading of and response to E.D. Hirsch's 'The Schools We Need and Why We Don't Have Them'. *Harvard Educational Review*, *69*(1), pp. 67–93.

Ceci, S.J. and Williams, W.M., 1997. Schooling, intelligence, and income. *American Psychologist*, *52*(10), p. 1051.

Clark, R.E., 1982. Antagonism between achievement and enjoyment in ATI studies. *Educational Psychologist*, *17*(2), pp. 92–101.

Egan, K., 1980. John Dewey and the social studies curriculum. *Theory & Research in Social Education*, *8*(2), pp. 37–55.

Freeman, S., Eddy, S.L., McDonough, M., Smith, M.K., Okoroafor, N., Jordt, H. and Wenderoth, M.P., 2014. Active learning increases student performance in science, engineering, and mathematics. *Proceedings of the National Academy of Sciences*, *111*(23), pp. 8410–15.

Garon-Carrier, G., Boivin, M., Guay, F., Kovas, Y., Dionne, G., Lemelin, J.-P., Séguin, J.R., Vitaro, F. and Tremblay, R.E., 2016. Intrinsic motivation and achievement in mathematics in elementary school: a longitudinal investigation of their association. *Child Development*, *87*(1), pp. 165–75.

Gehlbach, H., Brinkworth, M.E., King, A.M., Hsu, L.M., McIntyre, J. and Rogers, T., 2016. Creating birds of similar feathers: leveraging similarity to improve teacher–student relationships and academic achievement. *Journal of Educational Psychology*, *108*(3), p. 342.

Hastie, P.A., Martin, E. and Buchanan, A.M., 2006. Stepping out of the norm: an examination of praxis for a culturally-relevant pedagogy for African-American children. *Journal of Curriculum Studies*, *38*(3), pp. 293–306.

Hirsch, E.D., 2003. Reading comprehension requires knowledge – of words and the world. *American Educator*, *27*(1), pp. 10–13.

Hirsch, E.D., 2006. Building knowledge: the case for bringing content into the language arts block and for a knowledge-rich curriculum core for all children. *American Educator*, *30*(1), p. 8.

Hirsch, E.D., 2016. *Why Knowledge Matters: Rescuing Our Children from Failed Educational Theories*. Cambridge, MA: Harvard Education Press.

Kirschner, P.A. and van Merriënboer, J.J., 2013. Do learners really know best? Urban legends in education. *Educational Psychologist*, *48*(3), pp. 169–83.

Klassen, R.M., Perry, N.E. and Frenzel, A.C., 2012. Teachers' relatedness with students: an underemphasized component of teachers' basic psychological needs. *Journal of Educational Psychology*, *104*(1), p. 150.

Loveless, T., 2015. *The 2015 Brown Center Report on American Education: How Well Are American Students Learning? With sections on the gender gap in reading, effects of the Common Core, and student engagement.* Washington, DC: Brookings Institution Press.

OECD (Organisation for Economic Cooperation and Development), 2016. *PISA 2015 Results: Policies and Practices for Successful Schools*. Paris: OECD Publishing.

Perkins, D., 2014. *Future Wise: Educating Our Children for a Changing World*. San Francisco: Jossey–Bass.

Putwain, D.W., Becker, S., Symes, W. and Pekrun, R., 2017. Reciprocal relations between students' academic enjoyment, boredom, and achievement over time. *Learning and Instruction*. [In Press], DOI: 10.1016/j.learnin struc.2017.08.004

Robinson, D.H. and Bligh, R.A., 2016. An interview with Richard E. Clark. *Educational Psychology Review*, *28*(4), pp. 875–91.

Roorda, D.L., Koomen, H.M., Spilt, J.L. and Oort, F.J., 2011. The influence of affective teacher–student relationships on students' school engagement and achievement a meta-analytic approach. *Review of Educational Research*, *81*(4), pp. 493–529.

Rubin, D.B., 1978. Bayesian inference for causal effects: the role of randomization. *Annals of Statistics*, pp. 34–58.

Ryan, R.M. and Deci, E.L., 2000. Self-determination theory and the facilitation of intrinsic motivation, social development, and well-being. *American Psychologist*, *55*(1), p. 68.

Schraw, G., Flowerday, T. and Lehman, S., 2001. Increasing situational interest in the classroom. *Educational Psychology Review*, *13*(3), pp. 211–24.

Sherry, J.L., 2013. Formative research for STEM educational games. *Zeitschrift für Psychologie*, 221(2), pp. 90–97

Sweller, J., Ayres, P. and Kalyuga, S., 2011. The worked example and problem completion effects. In *Cognitive Load Theory*. New York: Springer. pp. 99–109.

Tyre, P., 2014. 'I've been a pariah for so long'. [online] Available at: www.politico.com/magazine/politico50/2014/ive-been-a-pariah-for-so-long.html.

Williams, E.C., 2016. *Taking the Wonder Out of Science Education.* [online] Available at: http://quillette.com/2016/02/20/taking-the-wonder-out-of-science-education/.

Willingham, D.T., 2006. The usefulness of brief instruction in reading comprehension strategies. *American Educator, 30*(4), pp. 39–45.

Willingham, D.T., 2009. *Why Don't Students Like School? A Cognitive Scientist Answers Questions about How the Mind Works and What It Means for the Classroom.* San Francisco: Jossey–Bass.

Yates, G.C., 2005. 'How obvious': personal reflections on the database of educational psychology and effective teaching research. *Educational Psychology, 25*(6), pp. 681–700.

5

EXPLICIT TEACHING

Key Points

This chapter will:

- Define explicit teaching
- Outline the evidence for explicit teaching
- Emphasise that the evidence supports using explicit teaching as a *whole-class* strategy
- Explain why explicit teaching strategies are supported by the science of learning
- Give practical suggestions for applying explicit teaching strategies in class

Lighting a fire or filling a pail?

One clear memory I have of training to be a teacher was when one of my lecturers spoke to us about Plutarch. Plutarch, he claimed, insisted that students were not empty vessels to be filled-up with knowledge but rather fires to be kindled. Years later, I investigated this quote. Not only did I learn that the meaning my lecturer had given to Plutarch's analogy was probably not the meaning that Plutarch intended, but that similar quotes have been attributed and misattributed to a wide range of thinkers. W.B. Yeats never said 'Education is not the filling of a pail, but the lighting of a fire', but that does not seem to matter.

The point my lecturer was making, and the point that is often made with such quotes, is that learning has to be active; it cannot be done *to* students. This is the essence of 'constructivism', the idea that students have to construct knowledge for themselves. This is an important idea; whichever way students learn, they approach new concepts with a wealth of ideas they have already acquired and they need to integrate the new with the old, sometimes overturning old or instinctive conceptions in the process. Students also need to actively rehearse new learning in order for it to be retained. All of this requires mental effort.

Yet constructivism is often taken further to imply that teacher-led classrooms are inadequate in some way; that students cannot truly understand something that a teacher explains to them and so they must be involved in working things out for themselves or with their peers. As we will see, this is not what the evidence shows. Teacher-led classrooms can be extremely effective. Humans appear to have evolved to be highly efficient at acquiring knowledge from others and integrating this with what they already know. In this chapter we will review some of the evidence for teacher-led, expository instruction and the most effective ways of implementing it.

Explicit teaching

Throughout what follows, you will notice that I refer to 'explicit teaching'. You may see this described elsewhere as 'direct instruction', but this label is ambiguous. Barak Rosenshine lists no fewer than *five* different meanings for 'direct instruction' (Rosenshine, 2008) which range from a term used to describe any kind of teacher-led instruction to a term to describe a specific set of programmes developed by Siegfried Engelmann and his associates in the 1960s – some researchers use the convention of capitalising the first letters to 'Direct Instruction' when referring to the Engelmann programmes (McMullen and Madelaine, 2014). Other meanings of 'direct instruction' are clearly used pejoratively and so I don't think this is a helpful term.

There are four defining features of the kind of explicit teaching that I will describe in this chapter. First, it is *teacher-led* with the teacher deciding upon the sequence of activities in a lesson. Second, complex tasks or products are fully broken down into their constituent parts and students are *instructed in the components* before being asked to bring them together. Third, new concepts are *fully explained* by the teacher to the students; children do not have to figure anything out for themselves. Finally, explicit teaching is *highly interactive* with *all* students required to participate frequently.

All of these statements would apply to the Engelmann programmes but such programmes take the model further. Lessons are scripted and are designed according to a set of principles set out in the book *Theory of Instruction* written by Engelmann and Douglas Carnine (Engelmann and Carnine, 1982). So these programmes can be seen as a specific example of explicit teaching more generally.

Note that the definition of explicit teaching that I am using excludes formal lecturing and default teacher-led instruction. Formal lecturing is not interactive enough and default teacher-led instruction is unlikely to take account of all of the key principles that I will outline below. In particular, it may not sufficiently and systematically

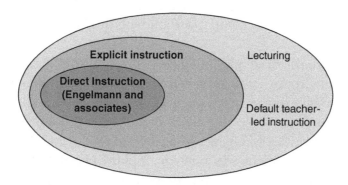

Figure 5.1   How explicit teaching fits with other forms of direct instruction

break complex tasks into their component parts due to a cognitive bias known as the 'curse of knowledge' that we will meet shortly.

Research background

Although as old as time, explicit teaching attracted a great deal of interest as a result of the process–product research of the 1960s and 1970s. In these studies, researchers would visit classrooms and attempt to code different teacher behaviours. They would then seek to correlate these behaviours with the learning gains made by the students in these teachers' classes in order to identify the practices that had the most positive effects.

It is worth noting that this kind of research can only identify associations. For instance, imagine that a research programme identified that teachers who had a detailed lesson plan had students who made the greatest gains. It may be that it wasn't the *plans* that caused these gains. Instead, the most conscientious teachers might be the ones who produce the most detailed plans and it was their conscientiousness in other matters – for example in correcting their students' work – that was responsible. As is often stated, correlation is not causation.

This should give us reason to pause and consider the possibility that simply copying the overt behaviours of the most effective teachers in these studies may not be enough.

However, if we can define a set of *principles* that link these more effective practices then we can see if training teachers in these principles leads to more effective teaching. Such training programmes were developed from the process–product research findings and they seemed to have a positive impact on students' learning (e.g. Good and Grouws, 1979).

So what are the principles of effective explicit teaching?

Good and Brophy (2008) identify a number of findings from the process–product research: teachers accept responsibility for teaching their students, e.g. they will reteach content if not understood; they create opportunities to engage in academic work; they have strong classroom management; lessons are rapidly paced but consist of small steps; the teachers actively demonstrate and explain concepts rather than expecting students to learn by reading texts or working on assignments; they provide opportunities to practise so that students master key goals; and they are pleasant and supportive.

Barak Rosenshine (2012) examined the same research and – unsurprisingly – derived a similar set of principles. However, in addition to reiterating the importance of presenting new materials in small steps, he added a few additional details: teachers should review previous learning daily; they should ask large numbers of questions; they should attempt to obtain a high success rate; and they should provide models, guide student practice and scaffold difficult tasks.

Both sets of researchers emphasise the need for regular reviews of learning – tests. These have something of a bad name due to the growth in standardised state-wide assessments and the political reaction to these. Yet Brophy, Good and Rosenshine promote regular, low stakes assessment, guided by the teacher, that seeks to identify the effectiveness of the teaching rather than to label students.

One particular piece of research demonstrates the findings of the broader research. Project Follow Through is an unfortunately named programme that is often seen as being a part of the process–product research even though it used an experimental design and, as such, probably represents the most expensive educational experiment ever conducted. It started out as an elementary school continuation of the US government's Head Start initiative for disadvantaged preschool children, hence the name. When the US congress drastically reduced the amount of funding available, Follow Through could no longer track students from the Head Start programme and so it was reengineered as a research study (Egbert, 1981).

Follow Through made use of a 'horse-race' design. Different models of teaching were developed and funded, and the performance of each model was compared with the others. The clear winner of the horse-race was the Direct Instruction model developed by Siegfried Engelmann, Wesley Becker and colleagues (Engelmann et al., 1988). This has been labelled a 'basic skills' intervention in the Follow Through literature because it did indeed emphasise basic skills. However, this seems to have led to the misconception that it had an impact only on children's basic skills whereas it had significantly positive effects on complex tasks such as reading comprehension and mathematical problem solving, as well as self-esteem (Bereiter and Kurland, 1981).

It is easy to criticise Follow Through because the study was big, messy and far from the ideal of a randomised controlled trial.

For instance, there was a great deal of variability between different centres applying the same model. So, it is quite possible to explain away the results. Based on longitudinal data, one group of researchers went as far as to suggest that Direct Instruction in early elementary school was linked to teenage criminal behaviour (Schweinhart et al., 1986). However, such a significant, long-term effect of an educational programme would be extraordinary, seems implausible and the statistical analysis that this claim is based upon has been rebutted (Bereiter, 1986; Kozloff, 2011).

One of the more interesting aspects of the Follow Through research is the number of people involved in education research who appear to be completely unaware of it. I think this tells us something about the relationship between the field of education and empirical, quantitative research.

Despite the disappointment they must have felt when the Project Follow Through results were largely ignored, Engelmann and his colleagues continued to work on Direct Instruction programmes and there are many available today, addressing a range of subjects and grade levels. These programmes have been the subject of ongoing research, with a recent meta-analysis finding consistent, positive effects that were statistically significant and moderate to large in size (Stockard et al., 2018).

The main body of process–product research was conducted in the United States but there have been similar studies in Britain and Europe with broadly similar findings (Muijs and Reynolds, 2010). Much, but not all, of this research has centred around primary classrooms.

Another interesting line of research that supports explicit teaching is that of strategy instruction. This evidence arises from a series of studies where researchers attempted to discover the thinking processes of experts when those experts completed complex or ill-defined tasks. For instance, the experts might be asked to think aloud while solving a physics problem. These strategies were then explicitly taught to students with some success (Rosenshine, 2009).

It is probably worth pointing out that there is a debate about the extent to which we should teach some of these strategies. Daniel Willingham has strongly argued that teaching reading comprehension strategies offers an initial benefit but reading performance is ultimately limited by vocabulary and background knowledge. If we focus too much on reading comprehension and neglect knowledge building then we will limit students' reading abilities (Willingham, 2006).

Moving away from optimal forms of explicit teaching, there is also a fund of correlational and experimental work that seems to suggest that default teacher-led instruction is superior to default versions of the alternatives. For instance, one review of data from the Trends in International Mathematics and Science Study (TIMSS) showed that teachers who used a 'lecture style' of science or mathematics teaching tended to have students who achieved more highly in these subjects than teachers who focused on problem solving and group work (Schwerdt and Wupperman, 2011).

Evidence from the Programme for International Student Assessment (PISA) shows a similar picture. A 2010 analysis of PISA mathematics results showed that 'teacher-directed' instruction was positively related to maths performance, although this relationship did become negative for high levels of teacher-directed instruction. Significantly, the same analysis found an overwhelmingly negative relationship between 'student-oriented' instruction and maths performance (Caro et al., 2016).

The survey questions that PISA uses to assess student-oriented instruction include questions about how often students work in groups, complete projects, help plan activities or are assigned differentiated tasks (Echazarra et al., 2016). So although the PISA figures do not provide overwhelming support for default teacher-led instruction, they do serve to caution us against the common alternative.

The fact that student-oriented instruction is associated with worse results is likely to be of concern at PISA because it forms part of its definition of good teaching (Echazarra et al., 2016). This may be why this finding has not been heavily publicised by the organisation.

Interestingly, a different set of factors that the researchers labelled as 'cognitive activation' correlated positively with mathematics performance in most states. Cognitive activation – making kids think – seems like an essential component of good teaching but it is a strange concept in the way that PISA defines it. Playing with the figures myself, I found that the answers to the different questions that PISA has developed to measure cognitive activation do not correlate very well with each other at a state level (Ashman, 2016). If anything, cognitive activation seems to be a measure of whether teachers are asking students challenging questions.

For the 2015 round of PISA testing, PISA placed the focus on science teaching. The study found that teacher-directed instruction was
associated with higher achievement in science. This time, it was con-
trasted with inquiry-based teaching, a similar set of concepts to
student-oriented instruction but placed in the specific context of science, including a focus on practical activities. Inquiry-based teaching
was associated with lower achievement (OECD, 2016).

The 2015 round of PISA also found that 'adaptive instruction' was
associated with higher science scores. This was based upon survey
questions that asked whether teachers made adjustments to lessons
to meet the needs of students, i.e. whether they sought and made use
of feedback. This therefore relates to formative assessment, a concept
that we will explore in Chapter 8.

All of the TIMSS and PISA studies relied on students' responses to
survey questions and so this, as well as the correlational nature of the
studies, needs to be borne in mind when considering the results.

A study in Denmark of the attitudes of school principals seems to
add support to this picture. The principals were asked about the
degree to which they agreed with statements such as, 'alternative
teaching styles are more important than traditional class instruction'.
The greater the level of agreement, the higher these principals were
rated on a scale of how student-centred their view were. This was
then compared with scores in a written mathematics test sat by students in the final year of school. The results showed that a
student-centred instructional strategy was associated with lower
maths scores, an effect that was particularly pronounced for students
with low parental education (Andersen and Andersen, 2017).

The final source of evidence for explicit teaching that I will draw
upon here is from the experimental research in cognitive science that
we reviewed in Chapter 3, the most famous of which is the worked-
example effect. In these studies, students are randomised into two
groups. The first group is given problems to solve and the second
group is given worked examples to study. The students who study the
worked examples typically perform better in a later assessment.

Worked examples here fulfil the role of an explicit form of instruction. The original studies look at algebra problems but the effect has
been replicated in a range of fields, including the use of an annotated
version of a Shakespeare play (Sweller et al., 2011).

It is worth noting a few details of this research. First, there is a
tendency to refer to this work as lab-based, as if it is quite removed

from school contexts, but much of it has been carried out with school students. Second, the effect fades as the relative expertise of the students increases and then reverses for experts in a particular field. This provides a clear justification for the typical sequence that explicit teaching follows; full guidance, followed by scaffolded work, followed by independent practice.

Whole-class

It is not hard to find references in the literature to small-group explicit instruction. The appeal is obvious; with a smaller group of students it is possible to leverage the advantages of explicit teaching while also more narrowly targeting the specific needs of individual students.

Unfortunately, most schools tend to ask teachers to educate students in groups of 20–30. If we add no additional resources then we are left with a trade-off. Teaching a small subgroup of the class will require a teacher to leave the rest of the class to work independently. Does the benefit of more targeted teaching outweigh the cost of less direct teacher input per student per hour of teaching? Probably not.

ORACLE was a British study of primary schools in the 1970s that largely followed the process–product approach. It was inspired by the 1967 Plowden Report into primary education, a report that had called for a change to a more progressive form of teaching that emphasised group work and hands-on activity. The ORACLE researchers looked to see whether these new approaches had spread to real classrooms and, if so, their effect (Galton, 1987).

Many teachers in the ORACLE studies attempted to manage the differing needs of students by allocating different tasks to different students and then instructing the students singly or in small groups. The researchers noted that the students who, at any given time, were not receiving input from the teacher were unlikely to be working in the most productive way. Some of the tasks teachers set these students to complete were relatively undemanding.

The effect of this unproductive individual work could be quite significant. Researchers at the University of Southampton examined the difference between mathematics instruction in England and Nanjing, China, where outcomes are considerably higher. They noted that children in the Chinese schools they studied were involved in whole-class interactive teaching for 72% of the time compared to only 24% in England (Miao and Reynolds, 2014).

Why does explicit instruction work?

Teachers certainly should be experts in the subjects that they teach. More knowledgeable teachers are able to see the bigger picture and can therefore explain the reasons behind the strategies they are teaching rather than simply giving a literal and procedural account (Wasserman et al., 2017). Interestingly, one common criticism of explicit teaching is that it is only useful for teaching basic facts and procedures, neglecting student understanding in the process (e.g. Tweed, 2004; McMullen and Madelaine, 2014). It is as if teachers are incapable of explaining concepts to students. Yet there is little evidence to support such a position. Whatever the instructional objective, be it basic skills or something as complex as utilising reading comprehension strategies, there is strong evidence for the effectiveness of explicit teaching (Rosenshine, 2009).

Teacher expertise is desirable but it comes at a price, one that is highly significant for educators. In Chapter 3 we reviewed a basic model of the human mind that consists of a constrained working memory and an effectively limitless long-term memory. We saw that the severe limitations of working memory can be overcome almost entirely when dealing with information held in long-term memory. And it is this effortlessness that perhaps leads us into error. It makes it difficult for an expert to empathise with the experience of a novice. Instead, experts tend to overestimate what novices know and understand. This phenomenon has been termed the 'curse of knowledge' (Froyd and Layne, 2008).

One way of overcoming the curse of knowledge is to use formative assessment strategies. We will deal with these in more detail in Chapter 8 but it is worth pointing out that a key focus of explicit teaching is interactivity. This is one reason why Barak Rosenshine suggests we ask plenty of questions and obtain a high success rate (Rosenshine, 2012). It may also be related to the apparent success of the strategies that PISA identify as providing 'cognitive activation'. It is this interactivity that is lacking in a formal lecture and this is why it is important to not confuse explicit teaching with lecturing.

Another way to combat the curse of knowledge is to break down complex tasks into component parts and teach these components before synthesising them. This requires teachers to analyse what these components are, something that may not be obvious to relative experts. For instance, many teachers will find the task of constructing an essay to be quite simple and will focus on what differentiates a good analysis from an outstanding analysis. They may then be dismayed to receive essays that lack paragraphs, include run-on sentences or do not provide evidence for the points made. Explicit teaching aims to uncover and demystify all of the processes involved so that students don't have to figure these out for themselves.

Probably most significantly of all, explicit teaching aligns with what we know about cognitive architecture. Not only have we likely evolved to borrow ideas of others and integrate these into our own minds, explicit teaching pays attention to the limits of working memory. By breaking tasks into their component parts, providing examples and explanations, we ensure that students only have to focus on one or two elements at a time. These can then be processed by the working memory and organised in the long-term memory. Explicit instruction aligns well with how we learn.

Practical strategies

Given the importance that I have placed on explicit teaching being *interactive*, it is worth discussing ways of doing this. There are two purposes to this interactivity. The first is to ensure attention – students who might be called upon at any time to answer a question are likely to concentrate on the discussion. This would suggest the inadequacy of a traditional model where the teacher asks a question, some students raise their hands and the teacher then selects one of these students to respond, because this model allows students to opt out.

Second, constant questioning allows a teacher to gain feedback on their teaching. Do the students understand? The teacher can then adjust accordingly, perhaps by reteaching a concept or trying a different explanation. We will explore the role of assessment and feedback in more detail in Chapter 8.

We can draw on the research for guidance on other practical techniques for boosting the effectiveness of explicit instruction. The next few suggestions derive from experimental findings in the field of cognitive load theory, a learning theory we first met in Chapter 3 (Sweller et al., 2011).

When I first started teaching maths I was in the habit of presenting a worked example and then asking students to complete a problem that required similar thinking but that was slightly different in form. I suppose I thought that this would help students transfer the concepts to other kinds of problems. Another common practice was for me to present a range of different worked examples before asking students to complete any tasks themselves.

In the original experiments that demonstrated the worked-example effect (see Chapter 3), researchers found that it was effective to pair each worked example with a very similar problem to solve. This probably works to ensure that students read the worked example and attend to its details. I now add this step into my teaching as it helps students consolidate the initial teaching. If some students don't achieve this – and many don't – then it is pointless asking them to apply the ideas to different variations of the problem.

This is a specific example of a more general principle: break the instruction down into smaller components than you think is necessary. The 'curse of knowledge' means that, as relative experts, we tend to miss stages out. So think about what they are and fill them in.

Another of cognitive load theory's 'effects' is the 'modality effect'. Although working memory is limited, it seems that it can be divided into auditory and visual streams that operate independently. Therefore, we are able to attend to more information at any one time if it comes as a mix of both speech and images. For instance, a geography teacher may project an image of sedimentary rock at the same time as discussing it.

However, if we intend to make use of the modality effect then we need to be careful of text and the 'redundancy effect'. Text on a screen or in an image can waste precious working memory resources if its purpose is redundant. For instance, imagine a slide with text on it that a teacher then reads aloud. Is the student meant to listen to the teacher or read the slide? If the text is exactly the same then there is no need for both forms of it but the student might find themselves reading a part of the slide that the teacher hasn't yet reached, causing a kind of interference. If the text on the slide and the teacher's speech are different then which are we expecting students to pay attention to, or are we expecting them to follow along with both simultaneously?

I often present students with slides containing text because I may then print these out for the students to refer to later. Now that I am aware of the redundancy effect, I build in time for students to read each slide as I stand there, silently. It feels a little awkward at first but I am used to it now. After I have given sufficient time – I tend to read the slide twice or even three times myself – I then start to talk about what it means.

Another peril with visual information is the 'split attention effect'. Consider the different ways we might represent a maths problem from the topic of trigonometry, as shown Figure 5.2.

In Figure 5.2, in the left-hand diagram students are required to look-up the values of a and b from a key below. This splits their attention between the diagram and the key, causing unnecessary cognitive load. When John Sweller and his colleagues initially tried to demonstrate the worked-example effect with geometry problems, they found that the worked examples were ineffective due to this problem. When they placed relevant information on the diagram at the appropriate positions (right-hand diagram), they were able to find a worked-example effect again.

Finally, a similar theory to cognitive load theory is Mayer's cognitive theory of multimedia learning (Mayer, 2014). This is concerned with the way that students learn from multimedia presentations. One finding of the research in this field is that students respond better to an animated person completing an example than to simply seeing the example. This may be to do with empathy and the ability of students to imagine themselves in the animated character. I think this has

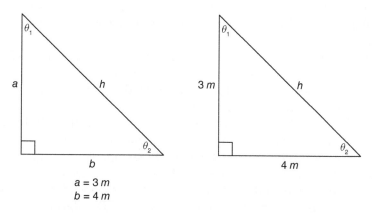

Figure 5.2 Examples from a trigonometry problem

implications for how we present in real life. Teachers should still work problems through in front of students, thinking aloud as they go, rather than simply presenting complete problem solutions or other forms of information. For instance, an English teacher might construct an exemplar paragraph in front of students rather than present a completed one.

Conclusion

Explicit teaching is not fashionable and discussion of explicit teaching is often omitted in favour of approaches such as inquiry learning. Moreover, there is a myth that explicit teaching is only any good for enabling students to recall basic information and that alternative approaches are needed to foster a deeper understanding. This is a shame because, done well, explicit teaching is a powerful approach that aligns with what we know about cognitive architecture. Once we accept this, we can focus on strategies for making explicit teaching as effective as possible.

References

Andersen, I.G. and Andersen, S.C., 2017. Student-centered instruction and academic achievement: linking mechanisms of educational inequality to schools' instructional strategy. *British Journal of Sociology of Education*, *38*(4), pp. 533–50.

Ashman, G., 2016. PISA proves itself wrong again. [Blog] *Filling the Pail*. Available at: https://gregashman.wordpress.com/2016/10/23/pisas-proves-itself-wrong-again/.

Bereiter, C., 1986. Does direct instruction cause delinquency? *Early Childhood Research Quarterly*, *1*(3), pp. 289–92.

Bereiter, C. and Kurland, M., 1981. A constructive look at Follow Through results. *Interchange*, *12*(1), pp. 1–22.

Caro, D.H., Lenkeit, J. and Kyriakides, L., 2016. Teaching strategies and differential effectiveness across learning contexts: evidence from PISA 2012. *Studies in Educational Evaluation*, *49*, pp. 30–41.

Echazarra, A., Salinas, D., Méndez, I., Denis, V. and Rech, G., 2016. How teachers teach and students learn: successful strategies for school. *OECD Education Working Papers*, No. 130. Paris: OECD Publishing.

Egbert, R.L., 1981. Some thoughts about Follow Through thirteen years later. Opinion Paper. Available at: https://eric.ed.gov/?id=ED244733.

Engelmann, S. and Carnine, D., 1982. *Theory of Instruction: Principles and Applications*. New York: Irvington Publishers.

Engelmann, S., Becker, W.C., Carnine, D. and Gersten, R., 1988. The direct instruction follow through model: design and outcomes. *Education and Treatment of Children*, *11*(4), pp. 303–17.

Froyd, J. and Layne, J., 2008. October. Faculty development strategies for overcoming the 'Curse of knowledge'. 38th Annual Frontiers in Education Conference, 2008. IEEE. pp. S4D-13.

Galton, M., 1987. An ORACLE chronicle: a decade of classroom research. *Teaching and Teacher Education*, *3*(4), pp. 299–313.

Good, T.L. and Brophy, J.E., 2008. *Looking in Classrooms*, 10th edn. Boston, MA: Allyn & Bacon.

Good, T.L. and Grouws, D.A., 1979. The Missouri Mathematics Effectiveness Project: an experimental study in fourth-grade classrooms. *Journal of Educational Psychology*, *71*(3), p. 355.

Kozloff, M., 2011. DI creates felons, but literate ones. *Contribution to the DI Listserve*. University of Oregon, 31 December.

Mayer, R.E., 2014. Research-based principles for designing multimedia instruction. Overview of multimedia instruction. Available at: https://hilt. harvard.edu/files/hilt/files/background_reading.pdf.

McMullen, F. and Madelaine, A., 2014. Why is there so much resistance to Direct Instruction? *Australian Journal of Learning Difficulties*, *19*(2), pp. 137–51.

Miao, Z. and Reynolds, D., 2014. How China teaches children maths so well. *The Conversation*, 26 September.

Muijs, D. and Reynolds, D., 2010. *Effective Teaching: Evidence and Practice*, 3rd edn. London: Sage.

OECD (Organisation for Economic Cooperation and Development), 2016. *PISA 2015 Results* (Volume II): *Policies and Practices for Successful Schools*. Paris: OECD Publishing.

Rosenshine, B., 2008. *Five Meanings of Direct Instruction*. Lincoln, IL: Center on Innovation & Improvement.

Rosenshine, B., 2009. The empirical support for direct instruction. In S. Tobias and T.M. Duffy (eds), *Constructivist Theory Applied to Instruction: Success or Failure?* New York: Taylor and Francis. pp. 201–20.

Rosenshine, B., 2012. Principles of instruction: research-based strategies that all teachers should know. *American Educator*, *36*(1), p. 12.

Schweinhart, L.L., Weikart, D.P. and Larner, M.B., 1986. Consequences of three preschool curriculum models through age 15. *Early Childhood Research Quarterly*, *1*(1), pp. 15–45.

Schwerdt, G. and Wuppermann, A.C., 2011. Is traditional teaching really all that bad? A within-student between-subject approach. *Economics of Education Review*, *30*(2), pp. 365–79.

Stockard, J., Wood, T. and Coughlin, C., 2018. The effectiveness of direct instruction curricula: a meta-analysis of a half century of research. *Review of Educational Research*, prepublished. DOI: 10.3102/0034654317751919.

Sweller, J., Ayres, P. and Kalyuga, S., 2011. *Cognitive Load Theory*. Vancouver: Springer Science & Business Media.

Tweed, A., 2004. Direct instruction: is it the most effective science teaching strategy? *NSTA WebNews Digest*. Available at: http://www.nsta.org/pub lications/news/story.aspx?id=50045

Wasserman, N.H., Casey, S., Champion, J. and Huey, M., 2017. Statistics as unbiased estimators: exploring the teaching of standard deviation. *Research in Mathematics Education*, *19*(3), pp.236–256.

Willingham, D.T., 2006. The usefulness of brief instruction in reading comprehension strategies. *American Educator*, *30*(4), pp. 39–50.

6

ALTERNATIVES TO EXPLICIT TEACHING

Key Points

This chapter will:

- Outline some of the objections to explicit forms of teaching
- Suggest reasons for using alternatives to explicit instruction that are consistent with the evidence
- Discuss the evidence supporting cooperative learning
- Describe approaches such as problem-based learning, project-based learning and inquiry learning and discuss relevant evidence
- Consider methods for differentiating learning
- Ask whether we are in danger of setting up a false choice between explicit and implicit methods

Making deposits at the bank

To many teachers, students, parents and policymakers, it makes intu-itive sense that it is not only more motivating for students to find things out for themselves, but that this will lead to a deeper under-standing of the relevant concepts. Yet in the previous chapters, we have not found a great deal of supporting evidence for this contention.

So should we conclude that it is best to use explicit teaching all of the time? Not necessarily. There are objections to explicit teaching that we need to understand and address and there are reasons for using the alternatives that are consistent with what we know from cognitive science.

Some of the objections to explicit teaching, while situated in the-ory, are almost visceral. This is a topic that people feel passionate about. It affects the emotions as much as the rational mind.

To some, explicit teaching is nothing short of a form of oppres-sion. It is perhaps Paulo Freire who makes this case most directly. In his popular classic *Pedagogy of the Oppressed*, Freire characterises explicit instruction as a 'banking model' in which teachers seek to make 'deposits' (Freire, 1970). He suggests that, 'In the banking model of education, knowledge is a gift bestowed by those who con-sider themselves knowledgeable upon those whom they consider to know nothing.'

This is clearly a mischaracterisation. To explicitly teach something does not require us to assume that a student knows *nothing*. However, such statements have great rhetorical power. Freire's alternative is 'problem-posing' education which attempts to meet students with questions and problems that are relevant to their own lives. Freire is writing in the context of a call for Marxist revolution. He quotes Mao Zedong and discusses the way that education can serve a revolution-ary purpose. Teaching methods – pedagogy – and politics seem to have become linked.

The question of *how* to teach can never be satisfactorily distanced from the question of *what* to teach. Curriculum is a vast topic but one criticism that resonates with many educators is a criticism of how we choose content. Like Freire, there are many who argue that a curriculum needs to be relevant to the lived experience of students; that it needs to recognise and respond to their communities and cul-tures. Descending upon them from a metaphorical height to teach them the canon, a corpus of work where white European men are overrepresented, is reactionary, conservative and disrespectful of students' own lives.

As educational theorist Michael Apple suggests (Apple, 1993), 'The curriculum is never simply a neutral assemblage of knowledge, somehow appearing in the texts and classrooms of a nation. It is always part of a *selective tradition*, someone's selection, some group's vision of legitimate knowledge'. This is undoubtedly true. So how should we proceed?

One answer is to let students partly decide on lesson content and this is facilitated by less directed, inquiry-oriented types of approaches. This is one reason why these approaches are favoured by many theorists. Of course, student decision making may be accomplished to varying extents. Teachers can give as much or as little direction as they wish. In some classes, students may choose how to respond to sources selected by a teacher; in others, they may generate their own questions to pursue.

A laissez-faire approach to exactly what knowledge students encounter is supported by the idea that, in the 21st century, all facts are available via the internet and so there is less value in simply knowing things than there used to be. Instead, we should foster students' critical thinking skills. However, as we saw in Chapter 3, such valued kinds of thinking require adequate reserves of knowledge in our long-term memory. Knowledge is literally what we think *with*. Critical thinking, something that all teachers wish to develop in their students, rests upon knowledge of the matter that you wish to think critically about. In the right contexts, small children can think critically and trained scientists can fail to do so (Willingham, 2007).

E.D. Hirsch makes a similar argument with respect to reading comprehension. The ability to comprehend what we read correlates closely with world knowledge. Writers continually make assumptions about what their readers know because to spell everything out in detail would make the writing tedious. So students need to be able to fill in these gaps and this requires world knowledge (Hirsch, 2003). Failure to teach this knowledge then becomes an issue of social justice because it excludes students from sources of information and disrupts their participation in democratic discussion. As Hirsch explains, 'If we tried to teach children a fully non-traditional knowledge set, they could not master the existing language of power and success' (Hirsch, 2016).

A similar debate is apparent in the field of science education. Deanna Kuhn (2007) argues that we need to teach more than just knowledge; we need to teach the skills by which knowledge is acquired. In science, this involves conducting scientific investigations and, again, this is prefaced on the idea that 'it has become next to impossible to predict what kinds of knowledge people will need to thrive in the mid-21st century'. It is as if knowledge is inert rather than something that is an active component of our thinking.

It is certainly a legitimate aim of science education to teach students about the scientific method and the strategies and equipment that can be used to complete investigations and this should involve students participating in experimental work. However, this may still be teacher-directed. The argument that teachers should stand back and let students make their own decisions in this context seems to be based upon a belief that there is a set of skills that we might label 'investigativeness' that will be enhanced through rehearsal. Or perhaps it is natural to assume that the best way to *learn* science is the same as the way that professional scientists *conduct* science. The case is not compelling (see Kirschner, 1992).

Nevertheless, there *are* some persuasive arguments for alternatives to explicit instruction. First, students who already have sufficient knowledge and expertise will gain little from having this same content explicitly taught to them. If anything, it could operate as a source of confusion. Instead, relative experts should either be learning new content at the edge of their expertise or using more open-ended methods to apply their learning to complex contexts. There is experimental evidence to support the latter approach in the form of cognitive load theory's 'expertise-reversal effect' where experts learn more from solving problems than studying worked examples (Kalyuga et al., 2003).

It is also worth remembering that the argument for explicit teaching is based upon its effectiveness at enabling students to learn knowledge and skills. What if this is not the aim? Perhaps we want to develop our students' positive disposition towards science. They may not learn a great deal from setting fire to corn chips but it is bound to be a lot of fun. The same is probably true for a game of historical celebrity heads; it may not be an optimal form of revision but it will mix things up a little and perhaps cut through some exam-related tension.

If students attend six lessons per day and in every lesson they are taught explicitly then this could be demotivating. I am not suggesting explicit teaching is inherently less motivating than any other form of teaching – I don't think that it is – but I do think that doing the same thing, all of the time, could be a problem, whatever that thing is.

Fortunately, a broad and balanced school curriculum necessarily contains a great deal of variety. It is tempting to suggest that art lessons allow students an escape from more directed forms of learning, although I am increasingly of the opinion that art skills should be explicitly and systematically taught. Nevertheless, drama is always going to provide the opportunity for group work and we must not neglect cooperative forms of learning in any discussion about teaching methods.

Cooperative learning

Cooperative learning – group work – does not sit well with fully teacher-directed instruction because the latter leaves little for students to cooperate on and discuss. Yet there is a substantial evidence base to show the efficacy of cooperative learning, particularly when compared with students working individually from worksheets and textbooks (Slavin, 1983). Cooperative learning seems particularly helpful when students are confronted with problems to solve (Slavin, 2004). There seems to be less evidence to demonstrate the relative effectiveness of cooperative learning when compared with explicit teaching but this is unsurprising because such studies would be hard to design fairly.

Since the 1960s, cooperative learning has been designed into the layout of many primary classrooms. It is rare to visit such a class today and find the tables arranged in rows; it would seem a little odd. Nevertheless, there is evidence to suggest that teachers don't use grouped seating arrangements in the way intended, focusing instead on setting individual tasks (Galton, 1987).

Robert Slavin has reviewed the research on cooperative learning and drawn out two conditions that are critical to making it effective. First, there should be a group goal that all students are working towards; perhaps all members in the group will be awarded the same grade or receive the same reward. Second, there must be individual accountability. Perhaps the teacher will select a member of each group to provide feedback but will not tell the group in advance who this will be (Slavin, 1989).

This second condition is necessary to counter the effect of social loafing, where individuals take a free ride while relying on others to do the work. Social loafing is a robust idea, having been observed in a range of different contexts (Karau and Williams, 1993). However, my favourite example is a quite wonderful experiment where people were asked to 'brainstorm' ideas. Groups tend to generate fewer ideas than the same number of people working individually (Diehl and Stroebe, 1987). There could be a number of reasons for this. Perhaps some people are less likely to air their views in front of others, or perhaps while Ali is listening to Jane articulate her idea, he is missing out on a chance to think up his own. Yet social loafing is also a strong candidate – why do the cognitive heavy lifting when others are prepared to do it for you?

Slavin's requirement for individual accountability circumvents this problem because everyone in the group has to be with the programme. If you are carrying a passenger then you better just hope that it isn't the passenger who is asked to feed back and who therefore harms the grades of everyone involved in the group.

It is not hard to find students who profess a dislike of group work. Sometimes they are introverts who simply prefer to work alone. Others will claim that they dislike collaborative environments because they end up doing all the work. If you want to lever the effectiveness of group activities then it is essential to set out the ground rules and bear Slavin's recommendations in mind. In my experience, few teachers actually do this.

Implicit teaching

The opposite of making facts, concepts and procedures explicit is to leave some of them implicit. This is what happens when we learn through discovery and inference. So 'implicit teaching' might be a good term to describe this approach, yet the expression does not seem to have caught on. Instead, implicit forms of teaching have many and various names, some exotic, others more commonplace.

At the time of writing, terms such as 'problem-based learning', 'project-based learning', 'inquiry learning' and even 'makerspaces' have become popular. Literacy teaching has its own set of labels, such as 'balanced literacy' and 'critical literacy'. 'Discovery learning' is currently out of vogue, as is 'whole language'.

'Constructivist teaching' also seems to be on the way out, with many now arguing that constructivist learning theories do not necessarily imply an implicit teaching approach (see e.g. Mayer, 2004; Hattie, 2009).

It is tempting to suggest that it is the relative ineffectiveness of implicit methods that makes it necessary for the frequent name changes. I couldn't possibly comment on that, but I do think it is worth exploring some of the more popular implicit approaches in order to gain a sense of what they do and do not involve and what the evidence suggests.

Inquiry learning involves students conducting an investigation in response to a prompt or question. It can be applied to any subject area but has specific features when deployed in science or history lessons. In history, students might use historical sources to attempt to answer a question such as 'How were Australian soldiers treated on their return from the Vietnam war?' A typical science inquiry may be to figure out which brand of paper towels can absorb the most water or how the length of a pendulum affects the time it takes to swing. In science inquiries, students are expected to follow the scientific method, perhaps choosing which question to investigate themselves, formulating a hypothesis, planning a method and controlling variables in order to run a fair test.

Notice that the objective of inquiry learning is to answer a question that is often quite complex and may draw upon abstractions. Knowledge will clearly need to be deployed in order to answer the question but the status of this knowledge is ambiguous; is the inquiry process intended to ensure that students gain this knowledge or is the knowledge simply a means to answering the question? Is the practice of inquiry perhaps an end in its own right?

To some, inquiry is intended to meet all of these needs in parallel. Inquiry learning is seen as a process whereby students 'learn content as well as discipline-specific reasoning skills and practices (often in scientific disciplines) by collaboratively engaging in investigations' (Hmelo-Silver et al., 2007).

It is worth returning to some of the potential pitfalls of relying too much on inquiry. As we saw in Chapter 5, evidence from the

Programme for International Student Assessment (PISA) shows a correlation between an increased use of inquiry approaches and lower PISA science scores. We cannot be sure of the cause of this; it could be that students who struggle the most with science are more likely to be offered an inquiry-style course, perhaps because teachers and schools think they will find this motivating. However, this correlation should at least give us reason to pause.

It certainly seems to be at odds with an understanding of cognitive science to assume that knowledge will be acquired in the process of completing something as complex as an inquiry (see Chapter 3). For example, in order to understand a source about how soldiers were received on their return from Vietnam, students would need to have some idea of why the soldiers were there in the first place, what they were doing and the political context in which this took place. And so we are reminded of Hirsch's argument about the role of background knowledge in reading comprehension. No doubt some students will already possess the required understandings but if we rely on this then we are designing an inequitable system where the more advantaged will continue to learn whereas the least advantaged will not.

So in order to run an equitable inquiry it is important to ensure that students have sufficient background knowledge of the subject into which they are inquiring, in advance. This is what happens in real life; when a physicist designs an experiment she may not know exactly what will happen in that particular experiment. However, she *will* know what has happened in a whole lot of similar precursor studies, she will know a great deal of relevant theory and she will be able to draw on this to make well-founded predictions about what is likely to happen. She is not operating in a vacuum, generating her hypotheses out of (very) thin air.

This speaks to a role for inquiry that sits towards the end of a learning process. Rather than *basing* learning in inquiry, it should work better as some kind of culminating task that builds on, and perhaps draws together, elements that have gone before. We will return to this theme later. In this sense, conducting an inquiry is much like writing an essay; it is a complex performance dependent upon skill in the numerous component parts.

Nevertheless, inquiry *questions* could be beneficial from the beginning of a unit of work. At this stage, such prompts can help build a narrative and give purpose to a topic.

Project-based learning is similar in many ways to inquiry learning. Here, the focus shifts away from answering a specific question to creating a product. However, if the product is a poster describing a history investigation then the two methods would become almost indistinguishable.

Project-based learning and the Maker Movement (Dougherty, 2012), its technological sibling, sound like the very essence of all that is bright, new and shiny in the world of education. It is easy to be lifted away on a tide of soaring rhetoric; up and out of the dusty schoolrooms of the past and into a bright future full of beanbags, learning pods and white hot gadgetry. Yet there is very little that is new here. William Heard Kilpatrick was writing about 'The Project Method' back in 1918, extolling the virtues of the 'purposeful act' (Kilpatrick, 1918). Many modern proponents would no doubt acknowledge a debt to the early 20th century philosopher John Dewey. It is reasonable to ask why this revolutionary method has not yet delivered the predicted results.

There *is* some promising evidence available from schools that have adopted project-based learning as part of a wider school agenda. For instance, 'Expeditionary Learning' schools incorporate projects, and reviews of the effectiveness of this model show potentially positive results (Borman et al., 2003; Comprehensive School Reform Quality Center, 2006). However, it is hard to untangle the projects themselves from other factors that vary between these schools and comparison schools. And, interestingly, the Expeditionary Learning model appears to use performance projects as the culmination of a unit of work, at least according to the curriculum units which are freely available online (Common Core Success, 2017).

The Education Endowment Foundation (EEF), a UK charity established to generate evidence on educational interventions and guide schools in the use of this evidence, conducted a randomised controlled trial of a project-based learning approach developed by the Innovation Unit. Twelve schools were assigned to receive the intervention and 12 comparison schools were not. The results were not promising, with the EEF finding a potentially negative impact of project-based learning on the literacy of students eligible for free school meals. However, five schools left the intervention, contributing to nearly half of the students in the intervention group dropping out before the final analysis (Menzies et al., 2016). This high attrition rate casts doubt on the security of the findings and raises the interesting question of why so many schools decided to leave the programme.

The other popular term for an implicit approach to teaching is *'problem-based learning'*. Again, it is worth stating that these labels are elastic and so the kind of mathematics teaching that is often described as 'problem-based' is also commonly referred to as 'inquiry learning' or even 'project-based learning' if tasks are distributed over a number of lessons. Further confusion abounds due to the common abbreviation for problem-based learning, 'PBL', being identical to that for project-based learning.

The defining feature of problem-based learning is that students are presented with a problem to solve. This is usually, but not always, more contained than a project, so a problem will typically be the focus of a single lesson or a part of a lesson.

In Chapter 3 we discussed the finding that relative novices generally learn more from studying worked examples than solving problems; a finding that does not bode well for attempts to base learning in problem solving. Nevertheless, the approach has proved popular with teachers and researchers and there are a number of studies that look at its effectiveness in different domains.

Jo Boaler, currently a professor of mathematics education at Stanford University, has run a couple of interesting studies that seem to demonstrate the potential of teaching mathematics through problems. The first study took place in England and compared two schools that she called 'Phoenix Park' and 'Amber Hill'. These two schools used very different approaches with Phoenix Park asking students to complete short projects based around interesting problems. Boaler found evidence that students at Phoenix Park developed superior conceptual understanding (Boaler, 1998).

Boaler then conducted a similar study in California, this time involving three schools. Again, one of the schools used a problem-based approach and Boaler found that this had some advantages over the methods used by the other schools (Boaler, 2006). However, it is hard to draw any definite conclusions from such studies because many factors will have varied between the schools concerned, not just maths teaching methods. This is why randomised controlled trials of school-based approaches typically use a larger number of schools than in the Boaler studies; recall that the EEF included 24 schools in its trial of project-based learning.

Problem-based learning has been widely adopted by medical schools for the education of nurses, doctors and other health professionals. For instance, students may be given a patient profile and list of symptoms and asked to figure out a diagnosis in groups, learning key knowledge and skills as part of the process. Helpfully, these methods have been subject to a significant body of research, which typically shows gains in some skills compared with conventional lecture-based university teaching, even if retention of knowledge is sometimes weaker for these students (Dochy et al., 2003).

Jerry Colliver, a researcher at the Southern Illinois University School of Medicine, has been critical of a number of these studies due to possible confounds and other problems in their designs (Colliver, 2000). For instance, in some studies it appears that the students in the problem-based learning group were more able than the students they were being compared with, possessing, for instance, higher grade point averages. In one case, students in the problem-based learning group had frequent contact with patients whereas those in the traditional group had far less clinical experience by that stage of the course. Both groups were then assessed on clinical skills. The positive result in favour of the problem-based learning students therefore seems to rely on what I have called the 'first principle of educational psychology': students tend to learn the things you teach them and don't tend to the learn the things you don't teach them.

We may also suppose that problem-based learning would help develop a general skill of problem solving. Unfortunately, general problem-solving skills appear to be biologically primary and so it is unlikely that we can gain them in this way (Tricot and Sweller, 2014). If we move away from academic outcomes then there appear to be positive effects of problem-based learning on motivation (Norman and Schmidt, 1992). Yet it is always going to be hard to untangle these from the motivational effects of being involved in a study or of having teachers who are enthusiastic about the new methods they are trialling.

Differentiation

Differentiation is the process where teaching and other instructional activities are altered in some way in order to better meet the perceived needs of the students. It is extremely popular among academics and policymakers, finding its way into national teaching standards (DfE, 2011; AITSL, 2017).

Many forms of differentiation can take place in an explicit teaching setting. For instance, some students may be given extension tasks or others may be offered additional scaffolds. Seating arrangement may be altered or the teacher may spend time with a group discussing a homework problem while the rest of the class complete a task.

However, some popular conceptions of differentiation are antithetical to explicit teaching. For instance, if students are grouped and given different tasks to complete in those groups then the teacher can no longer explicitly teach the whole class. The gain in greater personalisation could be outweighed by a loss in overall teaching per student. For instance, in a 60-minute lesson, a teacher could in theory teach the whole class for 60 minutes. If that class is instead divided into five groups then there is a maximum of 12 minutes teaching per group. This may be one reason why a large-scale study of differentiation in the United States failed to show a positive effect (Brighton et al., 2005).

I am also deeply concerned about approaches that seek to offer a range of options to students about how to complete tasks. There is evidence to suggest that the learning strategies that students most enjoy are not the ones that will lead to the most learning (Clark, 1982). Imagine a student who struggles with writing and who is given the option of recording a video instead. This may seem like a humane response but if this is maintained over time then the student's writing will never improve. Nevertheless, approaches such as these are routinely advanced as examples of best practice.

Rejecting a false choice

We need to be careful to not create a false choice when examining explicit versus implicit forms of teaching. We may picture explicit teaching as involving a teacher standing at the front of the room and explaining concepts, but an explicit teaching sequence should see students progress from emulation of the teacher towards more complex tasks and products. There are plenty of examples of poor practice but complex problem solving, essay writing and other synthesis tasks are always the ultimate objective. We are not bound by a choice between explanation and worked examples on the one hand and problem solving and creativity on the other; an effective approach will encompass both at different stages of the process. The relative lack of evidence for basing learning in implicit approaches is not because they involve complex tasks but because they omit explicit ones.

Conclusion

Ultimately, we wish students to be able to independently complete complex tasks and performances. However, this does not mean that we should ask them to do this from the outset because this is likely to be ineffective. Instead, we should follow a process of gradual release. In addition, there are other objectives to education than simply max-imising learning. For motivational reasons, it is worth considering the variety of activities that students are involved in and the opportunities that we create for them to work together.

References

Apple, M.W., 1993. The politics of official knowledge: Does a national curriculum make sense? *Discourse*, *14*(1), pp. 1–16.

Australian Institute for Teaching and School Leadership (AITSL), 2017. *Teacher Standards*. [online] Available at: www.aitsl.edu.au/teach/standards.

Boaler, J., 1998. Open and closed mathematics: student experiences and understandings. *Journal for Research in Mathematics Education*, pp. 41–62.

Boaler, J., 2006. How a detracked mathematics approach promoted respect, responsibility, and high achievement. *Theory into Practice*, *45*(1), pp. 40–6.

Borman, G.D., Hewes, G.M., Overman, L.T. and Brown, S., 2003. Comprehensive school reform and achievement: a meta-analysis. *Review of Educational Research*, *73*(2), pp. 125–230.

Brighton, C.M., Hertberg, H.L., Moon, T.R., Tomlinson, C.A. and Callahan, C.M., 2005. *The Feasibility of High-end Learning in a Diverse Middle School*. National Research Center on the Gifted and Talented, University of Connecticut.

Clark, R.E., 1982. Antagonism between achievement and enjoyment in ATI studies. *Educational Psychologist*, *17*(2), pp. 92–101.

Colliver, J.A., 2000. Effectiveness of problem-based learning curricula: research and theory. *Academic Medicine*, *75*(3), pp. 259–66.

Common Core Success, 2017. *EL Education*. [online] http://commoncore success.eleducation.org/curriculum.

Comprehensive School Reform Quality Center, 2006. *CSRQ Center Report on Middle and High School Comprehensive School Reform Models*. Washington, DC: American Institutes for Research.

Department for Education (DfE), 2011. *Teachers' Standards*. [online] Available at: www.gov.uk/government/publications/teachers-standards.

Diehl, M. and Stroebe, W., 1987. Productivity loss in brainstorming groups: toward the solution of a riddle. *Journal of Personality and Social Psychology*, *53*(3), p. 497.

Dochy, F., Segers, M., Van den Bossche, P. and Gijbels, D., 2003. Effects of problem-based learning: a meta-analysis. *Learning and Instruction*, *13*(5), pp. 533–68.

Dougherty, D., 2012. The Maker Movement. *Innovations*, *7*(3), pp. 11–14.

Freire, P., 1970. *Pedagogy of the Oppressed* (trans. Myra Ramos). New York: Herder and Herder.

Galton, M., 1987. Change and continuity in the primary school: the research evidence. *Oxford Review of Education*, *13*(1), pp. 81–93.

Hattie, J.A., 2009. *Visible Learning: A Synthesis of 800+ Meta-Analyses on Achievement*. Abingdon: Routledge.

Hirsch, E.D., 2003. Reading comprehension requires knowledge – of words and the world. *American Educator*, *27*(1), pp. 10–13.

Hirsch, E.D., 2016. *Why Knowledge Matters: Rescuing Our Children from Failed Educational Theories*. Cambridge, MA: Harvard Education Press.

Hmelo-Silver, C.E., Duncan, R.G. and Chinn, C.A., 2007. Scaffolding and achievement in problem-based and inquiry learning: a response to Kirschner, Sweller, and Clark (2006). *Educational Psychologist*, *42*(2), pp. 99–107.

Kalyuga, S., Ayres, P., Chandler, P. and Sweller, J., 2003. The expertise reversal effect. *Educational Psychologist*, *38*(1), pp. 23–31.

Karau, S.J. and Williams, K.D., 1993. Social loafing: a meta-analytic review and theoretical integration. *Journal of Personality and Social Psychology*, *65*(4), pp. 681–706.

Kilpatrick, W.H., 1918. *The Project Method: The Use of the Purposeful Act in the Educative Process* (No. 3). New York: Teachers College, Columbia University.

Kirschner, P.A., 1992. Epistemology, practical work and academic skills in science education. *Science & Education*, *1*(3), pp. 273–99.

Kuhn, D., 2007. Is direct instruction an answer to the right question?. *Educational Psychologist*, *42*(2), pp. 109–113.

Mayer, R.E., 2004. Should there be a three-strikes rule against pure discovery learning? *American Psychologist, 59*(1), p. 14.

Menzies, V., Hewitt, C., Kokotsaki, D., Collyer, C. and Wiggins, A., 2016. *Project Based Learning: Evaluation Report and Executive Summary.* London: Education Endowment Foundation.

Norman, G.T. and Schmidt, H.G., 1992. The psychological basis of problem-based learning: a review of the evidence. *Academic Medicine, 67*(9), pp. 557–65.

Slavin, R.E., 1983. When does cooperative learning increase student achievement? *Psychological Bulletin, 94*(3), p. 429.

Slavin, R.E., 1989. Cooperative learning and student achievement. *The Education Digest, 54*(6), p. 15.

Slavin, R.E., 2004. When and why does cooperative learning increase achievement. *The RoutledgeFalmer Reader in Psychology of Education, 1.* London: RoutledgeFalmer, pp. 271–93.

Tricot, A. and Sweller, J., 2014. Domain-specific knowledge and why teaching generic skills does not work. *Educational Psychology Review, 26*(2), pp. 265–83.

Willingham, D.T., 2007. Critical thinking. *American Educator, 31*(3), pp. 8–19.

7

PLANNING LESSONS

Key Points

This chapter will:

- Discuss the ways in which planning may have a negative impact on teachers and the quality of teaching
- Explain why effective plans work backwards from a desired learning objective
- Suggest that effective planning can help teachers reduce their own cognitive load when teaching
- Discuss ways of planning effectively across teams of teachers
- Bust the myth that textbooks are bad
- Explain how spaced practice and interleaving can be built into medium-term plans

When plans go bad

In December 1970, John A. Zahorik of the University of Wisconsin-Milwaukee published a paper that should cause anyone who has ever trained to be a teacher to stop and think. He had found evidence that, in some circumstances, writing a lesson plan was worse than having no plan at all. How could this be?

A large part of teacher training revolves around the production and subsequent evaluation of lesson plans. In my case, I was required to use a template supplied by my university. After teaching each lesson, there was a section to fill in where I could review the success of the plan. Plans were the main object of analysis in discussion with tutors and peers and, at that time, we were all too aware that Ofsted, the English schools' inspectorate, would ask for plans if they visited your school.

Indeed, planning seems to be a major component of teacher work-load (alongside marking). Based upon a 2013 international survey, the Organisation of Economic Cooperation and Development (OECD) estimated that teachers spend 7 hours per week planning. However, they also noted that this varies between countries, with the lowest average being 5 hours and the highest 10 hours. Regardless, even in the countries where teachers report the least planning, it still occupies a significant proportion of their working week.

In his study, Zahorik (1970) randomly assigned teachers to one of two groups with the intention that both sets of teachers would teach a lesson about credit cards. He gave the first group plenty of notice and the bones of a lesson plan that they were encouraged to further develop. For instance, he told them the objectives and detail of the content to be taught. He asked the second group to simply set aside some class time over the next few weeks for a task related to his research, without mentioning the subject of the lesson at all. *Seconds* beforehand, he asked these teachers to teach a lesson on credit cards.

Zahorik found something interesting. Those teachers who did *not* plan a lesson were more responsive to their students' needs during the teaching process whereas the teachers with a plan were more inclined to want to stick to it and ask affirmative questions of the students. Drawing on the discussion in Chapter 5, we might argue that the teachers without a plan were more adaptive.

Should we therefore abandon our lesson plans and busk each lesson as we see fit? Hardly. Zahorik had specifically chosen the topic of credit cards because teachers would already have plenty of knowledge. If you are teaching something less familiar then a significant proportion of planning time must be devoted to understanding the content yourself. The best piece of lesson planning advice I can give any aspiring maths teacher is to first attempt all of the questions yourself.

And good plans provide a framework that reduces your own cognitive load when teaching so that you may focus on the content. Teaching generates a huge amount to mentally attend to. Often we find that we are not just demonstrating something but also explaining what we are demonstrating at the same time. It is no wonder that new teachers can be a little overwhelmed by everything that they need to do and think about. I have lost count of the times that a class has ended, all the students have left and I have then remembered something critical that I forgot to say.

So even at this very basic level, a plan can be helpful. I use a PowerPoint template for all of my lessons and I can add tasks to this template that I might otherwise forget to complete; this can be from a simple reminder to check homework or take the register to a formative assessment task that actually *forces* me to be responsive to my students' needs.

Such plans will not necessarily look like the templates favoured by teacher training institutions and they probably will not involve spending the small hours trawling for second-hand resources on the internet. If you are reliant on either then I would suggest that you are doing it wrong. Instead, lesson plans should serve the needs of a busy teacher doing cognitively demanding work.

From finish to start

I am now going to make a statement that sounds obvious and yet has quite profound implications. When planning lessons, we should start by considering what we want the students to learn as a result. What will our students know or be able to do due to this particular lesson?

This principle is known as 'backward design'. It has been around as a common sense principle for a long time but it is probably Jay McTighe and the late Grant Wiggins who together did the most to popularise the idea in a series of books and articles they wrote (e.g. Wiggins and McTighe, 2005).

It *is* an obvious idea but, before you dismiss it as banal, I would point you towards the prevalence of the alternative: activity-based planning. This is the process of organising teaching around activities that you would like students to complete. Sometimes, this is because a problem or task is particularly interesting or you think it is likely to be motivating. At other times, there are reasons that are more prosaic: you already have a worksheet handy or there is a video-spaced hole in the lesson to fill.

Activity-based planning is not just a trap that busy teachers fall into – it is promoted at the highest levels. In her book *Mathematical Mindsets*, maths education professor Jo Boaler devotes an entire chapter to the design of 'rich mathematical tasks' (Boaler, 2015). She starts by describing a question that she asked of a group of Silicon Valley entrepreneurs: solve the problem 18 x 5 and show your method. The executives loved the problem so much that they even made t-shirts with 18 x 5 printed on the front. But what is it meant to achieve? What are people supposed to learn from this task? Boaler implies that problems like these make students excited about mathematics. I am not convinced but whether it is true or not, we need to be clear about what we want students to *learn*.

Sometimes, motivational aims may be appropriate. I used to run a science week where the chief objective was to show students exciting demonstrations. As long as teachers are explicit about this then it can be a legitimate goal. However, if I show students a cool scientific demonstration – perhaps one that involves an explosion – with the vague intention of the students learning some science then there is a clear risk. Unless I can articulate how that learning is going to occur then students may end up remembering a cool explosion happened and nothing else. In fact, the coolness of the activity might even work *against* the students' learning by taking up more of their attention than the scientific ideas.

Starting with the end in mind can clarify what we want the students to learn so that we select activities and teaching strategies that best suit this learning rather than starting with activities that may or may not be optimal. Nevertheless, working backwards is no panacea and there are two further problems that backward planning will not fix.

We might decide to look for short-cuts. This will happen if we focus on a finished *product* rather than knowledge to be learned and assimilated. Teachers may find themselves instructing students in heuristics that enable them to approximate features of the final performance. Imagine, for instance, asking students to use 'First', 'Second' and 'Finally' as paragraph headings or to ensure that their written arguments contain some arbitrary number of complex sentences. Such strategies might be useful aides-memoires when high-stakes assessments are due but they are not clear steps in the learning pathway. By focusing on the whole essay, we are focusing on too large a unit of analysis and not on something specific and defined. This problem will be explored further in the next chapter.

And starting with the end in mind can blind us a little to the value of consolidation and practice. If we interpret this framework to mean that students must always learn something *new* then we will prioritise novelty over mastery. I have heard people say, 'Once a child has shown that they can do something then you need to move on.' This is at odds with the science that suggests we need to continue to use it or we lose it.

Mitigating working memory limits

Let us return to the idea of teaching as a complex act. Imagine a typical situation where a mathematics teacher is demonstrating a solution to the class. Not only does the teacher have to keep track of the mathematics, they must also explain what they are doing at the same time. Add to this the fact that the teacher may wish to return some homework and arrange a time to meet with a particular student, and that the school requires attendance to be recorded in a particular way, and that while the teacher is talking there is a student in the corner who is chatting to a friend instead of listening, and the teacher was told this morning in briefing to clamp down on contraband jewellery ... When you first step into the classroom, you will experience a similar feeling to when you first attempted to drive a car: there is simply too much to pay attention to. This is the same cognitive overload that we met in Chapter 3 and that our students experience when trying to master complex tasks. And so the solutions are similar.

First, we want to make automatic as many facets of teaching as possible. Some of this will simply come with experience. Over time, teachers will start to automatically use classroom management strategies that they once deployed consciously, deliberately and with effort.

Most teachers have honed a 'look' that they give to students that applies just the right level of pressure. Sadly, this cuts both ways: if you practise the wrong things early in your career then these can be hard to unlearn at a later stage. I once attended a talk by Dylan Wiliam where he suggested that experienced teachers are doing well if they manage to incorporate *one* new formative assessment routine per year into their everyday practice because to do so requires us to deconstruct some of the routines that have been reinforced through repetition over time. Early career teachers should therefore reflect critically on the strategies that they choose to apply because these strategies will stay with them for a long time.

We may also consciously form routines to better manage what would otherwise be non-routine tasks. For instance, at the start of every lesson, I ask students to take out their homework books and place these on the desk before them. I then go around and check completion while my students complete a starter activity. Because this happens *every* lesson, I don't need to remember to do it. It is part of the routine. The principle stands even if this specific routine may not be appropriate at your school – I would remind you of my advice in Chapter 2 that you should seek out the implicit norms of your school so that you do not become marginalised.

Lesson plans also help by being a source of reminders. But it is no use adding a box called 'reminders' onto a lesson plan template that you will never actually look at during the lesson. This is why I prefer my reminders to be public – I add them to PowerPoint slides that will be displayed to the class. If the students can see the reminder then they might point it out if you forget to mention it, although I don't fancy your chances much if it is a reminder to 'Set homework'.

Another way of managing cognitive load is to ensure that you have worked out the key details in advance. That is why I advise new maths teachers to always attempt questions themselves before they try to demonstrate solving them in front of students. Sometimes this highlights gaps in a teacher's own knowledge and there is no shame in that. As teachers, we will regularly be confronted with obscure corners of the syllabus or approaches that we have forgotten about. In the latter case, we are likely to relearn these strategies much faster than our students can – that knowledge isn't completely gone; it's latent, sitting just below the surface and ready to be activated again – and so this is not a problem as long as we prepare well. However, preparation often just allows a teacher to notice key details and focus on an explanation of those details when teaching rather than focusing on the mechanics of solving the actual problem.

The same advice applies to *any* kind of modelling that a teacher may perform. If an English teacher decides to construct a model paragraph in front of the class then he or she should ideally attempt this activity when preparing for the lesson. This is not so that the teacher can then simply present the finished product and talk it through. Instead, the purpose of completing the task in advance is again to act as a rehearsal so that, when presenting the process to the class, the teacher can focus on the explanation.

However, once you have completed this level of preparation, it *can be quite tempting* to simply present the finished product and talk it through. We therefore need to be aware that some pretty clear evidence is emerging from the realm of multimedia learning – learning online from videos, animations and so on – that doing this misses out a key component.

Mayer (2017) calls this missing element the 'embodiment principle'. Researchers have conducted experiments where students are shown two versions of a video. For example, one version might show a presenter standing next to a diagram and explaining the physics concept of the Doppler Effect whereas the alternative video shows the presenter drawing the diagram as she explains. Students tend to learn more from videos like the second one and Mayer suggests that this is because the students feel more of a social connection with the teacher and mentally take part in the drawing of the diagram.

The joy of having many partners

We are now starting to develop a pretty long list of things to do in advance of a lesson. This is why lesson planning can be such a large component of workload. Part of the solution is to create space for lesson planning by using the more efficient approaches to marking that we will explore in the next chapter. Yet this is not enough. A first-year teacher faced with planning all of his or her own lessons from scratch will simply not be able to do this well and maintain a work–life balance.

There are therefore three options. The first is to give away any notion of a work–life balance. I do not recommend this. In fact, I suspect this is a reason why many new teachers leave the profession. Writing in the *Sydney Morning Herald*, one trainee who eventually dropped out from her course described how 'My husband cooked for me every night while I desperately marked student work and scrabbled together a plan for the next day, trying my best to cater for these oh-so-different young people' (Robinson, 2017).

The second option is to not be as prepared as you should be for your lessons. Again, this is not much of a strategy. Some people are able to busk teaching in this way but it is certainly not an approach for perfectionists. If you are going to thin down your planning then I would focus on meat and reminders. Throw out flashy activities and complicated lesson plan templates. In my experience, students rarely appreciate the activities that took 30 minutes to prepare and that are over in 5, preferring a good story over any intricately planned card-sort. Instead, make sure you know the content. A default lesson structure will help. So will a textbook.

A textbook represents a form of shared planning. And shared planning is the third and overwhelmingly best solution. Not only does it help with workload, it has a number of additional advantages.

Put simply, shared planning is the process by which you use another teacher's plan, on the understanding that you will supply them with a plan for a different lesson, perhaps in the future. Some school cultures are actively hostile to the idea. They valorise every teacher writing their own individual plan and often justify it on the grounds that teachers need to respond to the individual students in their classes, as if there are such vast differences between groups of students of the same age that one class will learn better from a completely different strategy to another class. There is little evidence for this idea (see e.g. Willingham and Daniel, 2012).

Other schools are more open to the idea of joint planning. In my view, the best approach is to coordinate this at a department level. Unfortunately, too many heads of department are so busy being leaders that they have no time for this kind of managerial task. In this case it is up to individual teachers to strike reciprocal arrangements.

Joint planning has another advantage. If two teachers use the same plan and one of them has a more successful outcome for their students in a particular area than another, it becomes much easier to pin down the source of the variation. If one teacher completes a group card-sort activity and another gives a lecture, then there are far too many things varying between the two activities to have any hope of inferring the cause of any difference. However, if two teachers have used exactly the same plan then it is likely that little deviations in this plan, perhaps in response to the students, have caused the difference. No, this is not a scientific approach on which we could base a research paper but it can lead to *good-enough* inferences that will gradually improve a school's approach to a particular topic.

You may notice the similarity between this idea and that of evolution by natural selection; generate small, random differences and check for fitness. This is how we create new knowledge when we have no prior knowledge to draw upon and it is in these small details, rather than in grandiose revolutions, that we can gradually improve our daily practice.

So my advice is to start your planning with what we already know from research – notions such as the embodiment principle – and then gradually, iteratively improve upon that.

Resources

I would like to return to the concept of textbooks because I feel that they have been much maligned in some parts of the educational community.

Some years ago, I was a deputy headteacher at a comprehensive school in London with oversight of budgets. The mathematics department had generated a huge photocopying bill and so I asked the head of mathematics to meet with me. Proudly, she explained that her department did not use textbooks, that this was something that had been instituted by the previous head of department who was something of a hero of hers and that she couldn't quite remember why he had done this, but if it was good enough for him then she intended to maintain the policy.

A brief visit to the mathematics department revealed that textbooks were not quite as absent as the head of maths suggested. Instead, ageing texts were surreptitiously stacked in little cupboards and hidden in teachers' desks. When asked about them, teachers would give furtive glances and try to read my face for approval.

The huge photocopying bill resulted from teachers reproducing pages from these books for use in class.

This reflects a practical reality: teachers cannot write all of their own resources. In mathematics, a teacher needs a source of questions that will 'work'. This is less important in subjects where questions tend to be a little more open and have prose answers. However, these subjects will have their own resource demands, such as readers in English, sources in history, practical worksheets in science, flashcards in languages and so on.

Textbooks are a valuable part of this mix. They are neither inherently good nor bad. Instead, the usefulness of textbooks varies depending upon alignment to the curriculum as well as the quality of the writing. In addition to use as a resource, textbooks can be a secondary source of instruction, a role that is often neglected.

When teachers abandon textbooks, they tend to replace them with photocopied pages from textbooks, worksheets or resources gathered from the internet. Often this takes place at short notice as teachers scrabble to resource their lessons for the coming week or even the next day. Is it really likely that these quick decisions made in the middle of a term will represent a better balance and mix, with superior sequencing, than the choices made by a professional textbook writer? Not only are teachers reinventing the wheel, the wheels that they are reinventing are not as well designed as the originals.

This phenomenon has seen the growth in resource-sharing sites where teachers sell their resources for a few dollars or pounds to other teachers desperate for something to use. Teachers should not be in the business of spending their own money in this way. Schools should be properly resourced with textbooks and other materials so that there is no need. As has been pointed out by commentators on social media (e.g. Theobald, 2017), the ethical questions about selling resources abound. If you produce a resource while working for a school then is it really yours to sell or does it belong to the school? Is it reasonable to make a minimal change to a resource that another teacher has made freely available and then sell this new version? I would like to see resource-selling services go bust as teachers collectively refuse to engage with them.

In a 2014 paper for Cambridge Assessment (Oates, 2014), Tim Oates makes a link between high-performing education systems and the use of textbooks. In high-performing school systems such as

Singapore's, textbooks are seen as a key part of the approach and are valued as an additional source of instruction. Curriculum requirements stay more stable over time, allowing publishers to iteratively improve their offerings and building a form of curriculum coherence across the system. In Shanghai, teacher-researchers offer 'adjustments' to the textbooks, with competitions held to feed the best of these back into the published books.

In contrast, Oates claims that there is an effective market failure in England where textbook quality is lower and focused quite narrowly on the requirements of terminal exams. This may have been why those wily maths teachers that I encountered as a deputy headteacher seemed to have copies of quite old texts. Perhaps these are our inheritance from an older and wiser age.

The role of cognitive science in a lesson sequence

Some findings from the science of learning – such as the value of worked examples – play out at the level of individual episodes within single lessons. We should be mindful of these findings when constructing these plans. However, other effects require us to be more strategic in our planning. Chief amongst these are the effects of retrieval, spaced practice and interleaving.

Retrieval, or the 'testing effect', was discussed in Chapter 3 and the main implication for planning is that we should build frequent, low stakes assessment into our lessons so that students have to practise retrieving valuable knowledge from their long-term memory. I repeat the caution from Chapter 3 that there is little point in retrieving something that is not there. If you ask students to learn a list of names then you can start retrieving that straight away but if you ask them to balance chemical equations then you first need to ensure they can do it.

Distributing retrieval over time is known as 'spaced' or 'distributed' practice. In experiments, this is usually compared with 'massed' practice. Cramming for a test is a form of massed practice because reviewing the material takes place over a short time. Distributed approaches attempt to split this up. Figure 7.1 is an attempt to illustrate the difference between massed and spaced practice. The assumption is that this will lead to greater retention over time and a variety of experiments involving students learning a

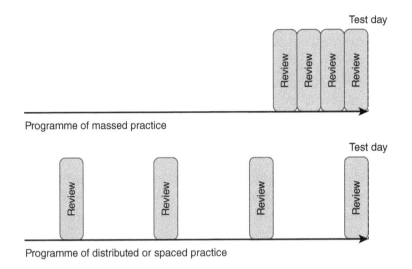

Figure 7.1 Spaced practice

variety of different knowledge and skills seems to support this idea, even if there is some evidence that the effects are lower for more complex material (e.g. Donovan and Radosevich, 1999).

The optimal gap between reviewing material – ideally through retrieval – is still the subject of research and likely to vary depending on the content. However, it is probably a good idea to plan to break up massed practice, provided, as in the earlier discussion, we are clear that the content has been learnt in the first place. A medium-term plan that allowed for little assessment until an end-of-topic test is one that will encourage massed practice. So you should seek to build in shorter assessments prior to the end of the unit – these have the added purpose of providing formative information and this will be discussed in the next chapter. It is also important to go back to material once a unit has finished, particularly if we expect students to be able to retrieve that content at a later date in an examination or as the foundation of a new set of ideas.

In some ways, interleaving is a very similar strategy to spaced practice and, in order to make full use of its potential, it needs to be present in medium-term plans. A typical practice schedule will involve students sitting down and reviewing one area at a time. Perhaps a biology student might answer a series of questions on the citric acid cycle. In an interleaved session, the student would instead answer one question on the citric acid cycle, one question on respiration, one question on DNA and then maybe repeat this process.

To an extent, answering past exam papers will achieve this aim but students rarely attempt these until late in a course of study. Proponents of interleaving would suggest that it should come much earlier; a soon as there are enough different areas to interleave.

Research on the use of interleaving in mathematics has shown quite large effects (Taylor and Rohrer, 2010; Rohrer et al., 2014) and this is thought to arise because it strengthens students' ability to match the correct solution strategy to a particular problem type. For instance, if you have just completed a lesson on how to solve simultaneous equations and are set a homework task on simultaneous equations then you already know which strategy you will need to use for each problem. If instead a number of questions require different strategies, then you have to work to identify which strategy to use. This will then help you with this identification in future.

Interleaving introduces a 'desirable difficulty' – you cannot simply use the same method to solve one problem after the next and so it potentially generates more thought. However, as with all such strategies, it is likely to be important that the content has been learnt in the first place otherwise we are simply increasing demands on students that are already high, particularly if the tasks are complex.

Conclusion

Planning is a vital part of teaching but not all planning is equally valuable. If we wish to make the best use of research into the science of learning then we cannot plan lessons on a just-in-time basis; we need to be more strategic. Efficient planning can help teachers focus on what is important in a lesson by taking away the need to remember lots of details or work things out in real-time. Yet planning is time-consuming and can easily take over the life of a new teacher. It is therefore important to draw upon all available resources such as textbooks and to collaborate with colleagues. You should also make time for planning by reducing time spent on other aspects of the work, such as marking–the topic that we will address next.

References

Boaler, J., 2015. *Mathematical Mindsets: Unleashing Students' Potential through Creative Math, Inspiring Messages and Innovative Teaching.* Hoboken, NJ: John Wiley & Sons.

Donovan, J.J. and Radosevich, D.J., 1999. A meta-analytic review of the distribution of practice effect: now you see it, now you don't. *Journal of Applied Psychology*, 84(5), pp. 795–805.

Mayer, R.E., 2017. Using multimedia for e-learning. *Journal of Computer Assisted Learning.* DOI: 10.1111/jcal.12197.

Oates, T. (2014) Why textbooks count. Policy Paper, Cambridge Assessment, November, pp. 1–23.

OECD, 2015. How much time do teachers spend on teaching and non-teaching activities? *Education Indicators in Focus*, No. 29. Paris: OECD Publishing.

Robinson, I., 2017. Our country needs good teachers. I am not going to be one of them. *Sydney Morning Herald.* [online] Available at: www.smh.com.au/comment/our-country-needs-good-teachers-i-am-not-going-to-be-one-of-them-20170629-gx15c4.html.

Rohrer, D., Dedrick, R.F. and Burgess, K., 2014. The benefit of interleaved mathematics practice is not limited to superficially similar kinds of problems. *Psychonomic Bulletin & Review*, 21(5), pp. 1323–30.

Taylor, K. and Rohrer, D., 2010. The effects of interleaved practice. *Applied Cognitive Psychology*, 24(6), pp. 837–48.

Theobald, J., 2017. Teachers: @TesResources has a problem and they want you to work harder to deal with it. [online] Othmar's Trombone. Available at: https://othmarstrombone.wordpress.com/2017/06/04/teachers-tesresources-has-a-problem-and-they-want-you-to-work-harder-to-deal-with-it/

Wiggins, G.P. and McTighe, J., 2005. *Understanding by Design.* Alexandria, VA: ASCD.

Willingham, D. and Daniel, D., 2012. Teaching to what students have in common. *Educational Leadership*, 69(5), pp. 16–21.

Zahorik, J.A., 1970. The effect of planning on teaching. *The Elementary School Journal*, 71(3), pp. 143–51.

8

ASSESSMENT AND FEEDBACK

Key Points

This chapter will:

- Define formative and summative assessment
- Explain what makes an assessment reliable and how we can ensure that the inferences that we draw from assessments are valid
- Link assessment to planning and teaching
- Give practical suggestions for generating useful assessment evidence and providing feedback
- Suggest ways of finding a standard to assess against

Doing tests

Tests are something we all do at school. Testing is also a political issue, with some groups of parents and educators organising campaigns to affect either the content of tests or the amount of testing (e.g. Adams, 2016). Some commentators believe that testing is stressful, a contributor to mental health issues and therefore inimical to their own educational values (e.g. Weale, 2016). The maths education researcher Jo Boaler has linked timed maths test to 'maths anxiety' – a kind of stress that affects mathematics performance (Boaler, 2015), although the evidence for this claim has been disputed (Simms, 2016).

Testing conjures images of young people sat in silence in draughty exam halls. However, this is just one, particularly narrow way of finding out what students know. Moreover, this kind of testing acts best as a form of *summative* assessment: it enables us to grade or rank students and summarise what they have learnt, often at the end of a course of study. This is an important function of assessment because it allows students and parents to evaluate how they are going and to hold a school accountable. However, it is the *formative* function of assessment that is the focus for teachers.

Dylan Wiliam is an authority on formative assessment, which he defines as assessment where 'evidence about student achievement is elicited, interpreted and used by teachers, learners or their peers to make decisions about the next steps in instruction that are likely to be better, or better founded, than the decisions they would have made in the absence of that evidence' (Wiliam, 2011).

In other words, formative assessment is when you *do something* with the evidence that it provides. It feeds back into the instruction – a form of feedback that is often neglected. The ways that assessment can do this range from asking a question in class before reteaching a concept that is misunderstood, all the way through to revising whole courses of study based upon evidence of strengths and weaknesses from formal assessments. It is the formal assessments – the tests – that we mostly think about when we think of assessment but it is likely that more fluid forms of assessment have as much, if not more, impact on improving the quality of instruction on a daily basis.

We should plan for *both* kinds of assessment, not just the formal kind. As we saw in Chapter 5, teachers suffer from the 'curse of knowledge' – a cognitive bias that leads sufferers to believe that a fact or solution step that is obvious to *them* is obvious to *all*. For their part, students may suffer from the Dunning–Kruger effect, where they underestimate the extent of their own ignorance because they lack the knowledge to recognise it (Dunning et al., 2003). Add these together and you have a vicious conspiracy against assessment: teachers do not assess the obvious and students don't realise that they don't know it.

By planning for assessment, you short-circuit this problem. If a teacher is constantly confronted with the evidence of his or her students' lack of understanding then this will puncture the curse of knowledge. This assessment evidence will also help counter the Dunning–Kruger effect in students although we must take care about how it is used. As we have seen, motivation builds on self-concept and self-efficacy. This is why Barak Rosenshine advises us to obtain a high success rate (Rosenshine, 2012). If we constantly point out a student's weaknesses then this will likely be demotivating.

So the unvarnished truth is more the teachers' burden to bear, within the bounds of honesty and accountability. And this is largely as it should be. Students should be focused on the next incremental step towards mastery (Bandura and Schunk, 1981). It is for teachers to see the wider terrain and plan a route through it.

Much of the current political discussion of 'testing' suggests that it may be stressful for students and contribute to wider mental health issues (Weale, 2016). I am sure that this *can* be the case. I am also certain that skilful teachers will present assessment to their students in a calm, positive and supportive way: 'This will help us figure out what you need next. It's no big deal.'

Some schools lack a strategy for improving the levels of literacy and numeracy: subjects that are often the target of standardised testing. In these instances, it may be tempting to simply push students through lots of practice tests with the hope that they will somehow learn how to complete them implicitly. Yet, as we have seen, implicit forms of learning are not optimal unless students already possess a great deal of expertise. A small amount of practice testing is clearly desirable because it will help students to become familiar with the format, but overdoing it is likely to raise the profile of the standardised test as a big, scary event that teachers appear concerned about, while doing relatively little to improve students' performance.

Instead, the solution lies in more frequent, low-stakes assessment that targets specific learning objectives and links to identifiable teaching strategies. If the only teaching strategy that we can think of is to ask students to practise doing it, then we have it badly wrong.

The concepts of *reliability* and *validity* are useful in understanding how different types of assessment function and the decisions that we need to make when selecting assessment tools.

Reliability

Reliability is the extent to which a person possessing the same knowledge, sitting the same test, will receive the same outcome each time. This is crucial for high-stakes systems where educational and career pathways are dependent upon the outcomes of tests. It would not be desirable for students with similar knowledge of a subject area to receive wildly different scores.

You might think this is an easy problem to solve but we need to consider the fact that formal tests only ever *sample* a body of knowledge. The subjects that we teach in school contain so much content that a test writer cannot possibly assess all of it. If an assessment focuses a great deal on an obscure corner of the course then it is unlikely to be reliable because students with a similar level of performance across the subject *as a whole* may differ in their recall and understanding of this little corner. Test writers therefore need to take care to sample across the range of subject matter and often hone certain types of question that generate reliable responses.

Three implications of this should be apparent to a teacher seeking formative information. First, to some extent teachers *can* assess the entire course rather than sample it. Second, a teacher's main aim is not to judge or rank students across an entire course but to seek improvements wherever they may lie. Third, a test question that a test designer has written in order to produce reliable outcomes will not necessarily be the best question to elicit formative information; these two objectives are different.

One way to illustrate this problem is to consider a multiple-choice question. Imagine the following mathematics question:

Which of the following shows 0.35 ÷ 0.5 in its most simplified form?

A. $\dfrac{35}{50}$ 　　　　 B. $\dfrac{7}{10}$ 　　　　 C. $\dfrac{3}{5}$ 　　　　 D. $\dfrac{17}{25}$

A standardised test designer might write such a question, trial it and find it to be reliable. However, a maths teacher is likely to be disappointed with this question because it misses an opportunity to test for a key misconception. Many students struggle with the value of different digits in decimals and will equate $0.35 \div 0.5$ with $\frac{35}{5}$ or 7. Therefore, including this option as one of the answers will generate useful formative evidence. If large numbers of students select it, we know what to target next in our teaching.

Moreover, imagine this question is included in an assessment task that asks students to rank the following numbers in order of size: 0.24, 0.6, 0.58, 0.2. This question would be harder for a standardised test designer to assign a score. However, it assesses the same key misconception and will therefore provide additional evidence to the teacher.

In my experience, many schools start their assessment journey by analysing the outcomes of external tests. This is fine as far as it goes, but we must recognise the limitations; these tests have been designed to assess reliably rather than to provide us with information.

Validity

Unlike reliability, validity is not a property of the test itself, even if a lack of reliability can harm validity. Validity is about the *inferences* that we draw from an assessment. Does the assessment support the inferences that we have made?

To illustrate this difference, consider a learning styles assessment. This is not an assessment of knowledge and understanding but a tool designed to elicit a person's preferred learning style. Nonetheless, the concepts of reliability and validity still apply.

For instance, there is evidence that some learning style assessments are reasonably reliable (Coffield et al., 2004).The same student will be allocated the same learning style on repeated assessments. What should we do with such information? Well, one idea might be to try to teach curriculum content in the students' preferred learning styles.

Yet there is little evidence to support the idea that teaching students in their preferred learning style leads to improved performance (Pashler et al., 2008). Some have argued that labelling students in this way can be detrimental and create a negative self-perception (Dinham, 2016). It would therefore not be valid to infer from this assessment that we should teach a student in a particular way.

We may also illustrate the concept of validity by a more commonplace example. Imagine that we ask a student to write an extended argument – an essay, for instance. The essay contains a number of run-on sentences – a stylistic error. It would be tempting to infer that the student does not understand the concept of a run-on sentence and needs to be taught this concept.

However, knowing the form of a run-on sentence is declarative knowledge (knowing *that*) whereas avoiding run-on sentences in your own writing is procedural knowledge (knowing *how*). The evidence is only enough to suggest that there might be a problem with procedural knowledge in this case. And we can't even be sure about that.

Writing is an intensely complex process with a high cognitive load. At any one time, a writer has many different items to attend to (Kellogg, 2006). Perhaps the student possesses declarative knowledge of run-on sentences *and* procedural knowledge of run-on sentences but has failed to put this knowledge into practice. This might be because he or she was too busy thinking about the ideas in the argument, the structure of the argument, spelling, punctuation or all manner of other things.

In this case, our inferences about the student's knowledge of run-on sentences would not be valid. Incidentally, this is the main reason why complex performances such as whole pieces of writing, completed projects, drama productions and so on rarely yield useful formative information.

Linking planning and assessment

In the previous chapter we saw that a plan should work back from a learning objective. The role of assessment is to provide information about progress towards such learning objectives and so planning and formative assessment form part of a loop, they must connect to each other.

It seems an obvious point to make, but how can we draw inferences about teaching if we have not taught the concept that we are assessing? At best, this information may set a baseline but, at worst, it provides little useful evidence. Similarly, imagine assessing something that we have no idea how to teach. This is not as far-fetched as it may appear. For instance, the skill we are assessing might be something that we expect students to develop implicitly. If so, such an assessment will tell us if students have acquired the skill but will give us little information about what to do if they have not.

Rather than plan a topic and then think about how to assess it at the end, we need to build formative assessment processes into our planning. This assessment must link back to specific sequences of teaching so that we can evaluate the impact *of that teaching*. We can then adjust course with current students if necessary and perhaps revise our plan for the next group of students.

Notice that this use of assessment is different to the instructional uses of assessment – spaced practice and retrieval practice – that we discussed in the previous chapter. The purpose of formative assessment is to draw inferences from the information that you collect whereas the purpose of instructional assessment is to support the learning process. However, an assessment timed to occur several weeks after the relevant teaching could provide both instructional support *and* information about how the relevant concepts have been retained.

Breaking down complex tasks

Complex performances are hard to draw inferences from because they require the interaction of content knowledge with a range of skills and therefore impose a high cognitive load for novice learners. Too often, teachers launch students into complex performances that are information rich but inference poor. As we have seen, a piece of writing might contain run-on sentences, grammatical errors, confused ideas, evidence that does not support the point being made or any number of other flaws and yet we cannot be sure of the reasons why.

One way that many teachers try to deal with this is by writing lots of 'feedback' at the end of the piece of work. It is unfortunate that so many teachers and school leaders have conflated the notion of providing feedback with writing comments in this way. It means that they interpret evidence for the positive effects of feedback, for example as presented in Hattie's influential book *Visible Learning* (Hattie, 2008), as evidence for this kind of marking when it almost certainly is not.

It seems unlikely that students will be able to process all of the information that a teacher provides in this way due to the cognitive load that this would generate. Even if they can, some of this will be redundant. For example, a student who makes grammatical errors due to the demands of the task but who can recognise these errors in isolation does not need to be told that these are grammatical errors. Compounding these problems, many teachers are encouraged to provide feedback based upon a rubric that is intended to be generic and this prompts generic feedback such as, 'in order to improve you need to develop your ideas more fully'. This may be true but it is hardly helpful.

Where rubrics highlight more specific details we run a different risk. According to Australian researcher Royce Sadler (Sadler, 2009) there are at least 50, and probably more, criteria on which to judge a piece of writing. By highlighting just a few and prompting students to pay attention to these features we risk encouraging form over substance. For instance, it may *generally* be true that good writing contains two or more complex sentences but by simply training students to produce two or more complex sentences, we will not guarantee good writing.

Not only is this kind of feedback likely to be ineffective, it is punishing for teachers. Writing comments is time-consuming and inefficient compared to simply speaking to a student. For instance, a quick test shows that I can say 'The quick brown fox jumps over the lazy dog' in about 2 seconds, whereas it takes me 15 seconds to write it down. As Dylan Wiliam asks (Wiliam, 2011), 'Does the teacher get the class's learning back on track with the class in front of him, in one go, and when the meanings of students' responses and the teacher's questions

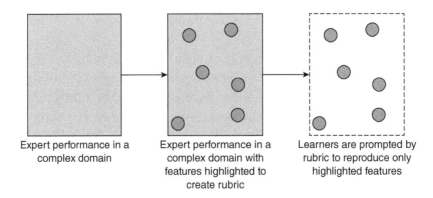

Expert performance in a complex domain

Expert performance in a complex domain with features highlighted to create rubric

Learners are prompted by rubric to reproduce only highlighted features

Figure 8.1   How rubrics fail

can be negotiated, or does the teacher do it one student at a time, after they have gone away, and in writing?'

Imagine a soccer coach who used a similar approach with her team. Every training would involve a practice game of soccer. At the end of every session she would then write a note to each of her players containing advice on various aspects of their performance and what to work on next. She would give these notes out at the start of the next training session. This is not, of course, how real soccer coaches work. They constantly intervene and provide verbal feedback. They gather players together and explicitly instruct them in some aspect of play.

Crucially, the repertoire of soccer training activities extends way beyond simply playing practice games. This is important because real games are unpredictable. If you want your players to improve a particular skill then you need to develop a discrete activity that targets that skill. You do not wait for the need for this skill to occur serendipitously and fleetingly in the context of a game.

Similarly, a more productive route for teachers is to break complex performances down into components that deal with specific knowledge and skills. Teachers may then provide feedback that is specific to that component and that is likely to be understood by the student who is then able to link it to that context.

The simplest way to do this is through a separation in time. If doing a number of things simultaneously will lead to cognitive overload then why not try doing them sequentially? In the case of writing, an obvious example is to have a discrete period of writing followed by a discrete period of proofreading. For instance, a student might produce an essay for homework and bring it to class. The teacher could then give over the first 20 minutes of class to proofreading the work and editing it. At least, this way, the teacher will not be faced with correcting errors that the student could have corrected herself.

If a student is writing a response to a text then one component that teachers should assess is knowledge and understanding of the text. If a student has not read the text or has misunderstood it then she will not write a good response. One way to check for this is to ask a short multiple-choice quiz. The teacher can then go through the quiz while each student assesses their own answers. If a student performs well then we know that a later lack of clarity in the complex product is not due to the student's understanding of the text. We have systematically ruled that out.

Similarly, we could design assessment tasks where students identify or generate topic sentences, distinguish sentences that analyse
from those that summarise or select appropriate evidence to support a particular point. If we know that students can successfully
complete these tasks in isolation and we also know that they have
the relevant content knowledge then we know that a failure to put
them together in a complex performance is down to the cognitive
load generated by manipulating them together. The response we
would then give in this situation will not be to explain what a topic
sentence is.

Teaching is a more efficient way of providing feedback than writing
to all of your students and so this should be a primary method.
Perhaps your students might complete an introductory paragraph
which they hand in at the end of the lesson. Rather than writing comments on all of them, a more efficient approach would be to simply
read them and address the issues raised in a segment of explicit
teaching at the start of the next lesson. You may then move on to a
period of redrafting where the students can respond to this feedback.
Dylan Wiliam calls this kind of routine an 'exit pass question'
(Wiliam, 2011).

I have had discussions with colleagues about these ideas, and
English teachers, in particular, find them deeply uncomfortable. It is
as if they see marking as some form of penitential devotional act. They
worry that a lack of red pen on their students' work will signal that
they do not care. Yet when they try out some of these approaches, they
often comment that the students did not seem to mind and quite liked
the new modes of feedback. This is understandable; if the feedback is
efficient then it will help students make progress that, in turn, will
increase their motivation.

If you are convinced by this argument then you may come up
against a problem when you want to enact it at school. Many
schools or departments have marking policies that mandate a certain, often unreasonable, amount of written feedback. Some have
even adopted strange policies where students have to write odd little replies to the written feedback they receive. This seems to be a
corruption of the perfectly reasonable idea that feedback has to be
taken on board by the student in order to have any effect and this
ritual is somehow intended to demonstrate that it has been. I have

even heard of policies that ask teachers to *write down* the verbal feedback that they have given to students, thus eliminating and reversing the efficiency gains of providing verbal feedback.

It is therefore worth asking a school about its marking policy on interview. Like a lack of a behaviour policy, an absurd marking policy should act as a potential deal-breaker.

Feedback to the teacher

A related problem arises from conflating feedback with marking. One of the most powerful influences of feedback is when feedback is provided *to the teacher* (Hattie, 2008). If we lock ourselves into a cycle of asking for complex performances before providing 'feedback' on these performances then we are reflecting only on the relative strengths of our students. If a reflection on the quality of teaching comes into this *at all* then it is likely to be as an expression of frustration that those pesky teachers who taught our students in previous years didn't manage to fix their grammar issues, teach them their times-tables or inspire them with enough 'ideas'.

On the other hand, imagine selecting a key issue to address, such as the quality of topic sentences, then planning an episode where you intentionally and explicitly teach students how topic sentences work and what distinguishes good ones from bad ones. When you read the topic sentences that students later write for a component assessment you can draw inferences about the effectiveness of this teaching. It gives you agency. You start to get a feel for what works and what does not. You build a repertoire of examples, analogies and explanations that you can directly link to changes in student performance.

Finding a standard

Suppose you ask students a biology question and the average mark out of 4 is 2.3. How concerned should you be?

In one sense, it does not matter. This question-level data has enabled you to discover something that your students cannot reliably do and so this is potentially formative information.

If the question comes from a standardised test then you might be able to glean additional helpful data. For instance, the country or state might publish the average scores for each question across the entire cohort so you can compare your students' scores with this cohort score. If the cohort score is 3.3 out of 4 then you might want to prioritise the concepts assessed by this question and perhaps generate some more instructional and formative assessment tasks that target these same concepts. If the cohort score is 1.2 out of 4 then your students have done pretty well in comparison to the cohort. It might simply be the case that this kind of question is particularly difficult or maybe it is badly designed with confusing wording.

This illustrates the value of having some kind of standard to measure against. It enables you to prioritise the concepts to address most urgently and it gives you a sense of the level of performance that we might typically expect of students studying the same content. If your students are from similar backgrounds to the cohort average then you might even be able to draw some loose inferences about the relative effectiveness of your teaching in particular areas. If not, then over time you might get a feel for how your students generally track against this cohort and look for areas where this pattern breaks down.

Unfortunately, many subject areas and year levels have no standardised testing to draw upon. In this case, there are two alternative ways of establishing some kind of standard.

The first method is to run the same, or a very similar, assessment in successive years. This is a strong way of establishing the progress of a teaching programme over time. You can look at changes you have made in one year and infer whether they have had an effect. This works well for small schools or elective subjects where there is only one class at each year level. One drawback is that it takes at least a year to establish a standard. In addition, any change to the curriculum will make it hard to reuse assessments. In my experience, politicians and school leaders are endlessly 'innovating' with the curriculum and so this is a major issue. Nevertheless, if you cannot rerun an assessment in its entirety then you may be able to run parts of it. This another reason why it is essential to collect data at the level of performance on individual questions rather than just a total for the assessment.

If more than one teacher is teaching the same course to the same year group of students, then there is the potential to compare data between those groups. This can be a little confronting for teachers but, provided nobody gets hanged, after a while a team will build up enough trust for this to work well. Even if the groups are not evenly matched in their prior achievement, you can still draw useful inferences. For instance, we may expect a lower-achieving group to generally underperform a higher one, but what of those questions where the pattern is reversed? How did the teaching of those concepts differ?

In many schools the answer will be: in lots of different ways. Teacher A taught the causes of the First World War using a card-sort activity with students grouped at tables before reporting to the class whereas Teacher B used a more direct approach involving chalk and talk. It is hard to work out what has potentially caused any difference. Yet if teachers plan jointly, as described in the previous chapter, then the ways that different classrooms vary will be more limited and so this offers the potential to zero-in on specific examples, explanations or strategies that may have been more effective.

In my own maths department, I recall a discussion where it was clear that the students in one teacher's class had outperformed the students in the other classes on a particular question type. All the teachers were using the same resources and same examples. When asked, the successful teacher could not think of anything that he had done differently. Finally, we asked him to stand at the front and show us how he had taught a specific example. In turned out that he was inserting an addition step into the solution method, the benefits of which were immediately obvious to the other teachers, so we wrote that step into the materials for *every* class for the following year.

Conclusion

Assessment is not testing; it is much broader than that and includes everything from asking questions in class to sitting formal examinations. The primary goal of most of the assessment conducted by teachers is to draw valid inferences that will feed back in to teaching in some way. This includes everything from identifying needs to address with a particular student or class to tweaking or completely redesigning teaching sequences for future groups of students.

Feedback is not marking; it is much broader than that and can often be accomplished more efficiently by giving feedback on common issues to groups of students rather than individually and in writing. Feedback also includes the notion of feedback *to the teacher*. Unless teachers can connect assessment evidence to an episode of teaching then it is not very helpful in improving the effectiveness of teachers.

References

Adams, R., 2016. Parents and children take part in boycott of primary school tests. *The Guardian*, 3 May. [online] Available at: www.theguardian.com/education/2016/may/03/sats-tests-parents-children-boycott-primary-school-exams.

Bandura, A. and Schunk, D.H., 1981. Cultivating competence, self-efficacy, and intrinsic interest through proximal self-motivation. *Journal of Personality and Social Psychology*, *41*(3), p. 586.

Boaler, J., 2015. *Mathematical Mindsets: Unleashing Students' Potential through Creative Math, Inspiring Messages and Innovative Teaching.* Hoboken, NJ: John Wiley & Sons.

Coffield, F., Moseley, D., Hall, E. and Ecclestone, K., 2004. Learning styles and pedagogy in post-16 learning: a systematic and critical review. Learning and Skills Research Centre. Available at: www.leerbeleving.nl/wp-content/uploads/2011/09/learning-styles.pdf.

Dinham, S., 2016. Students are not hard-wired to learn in different ways – we need to stop using unproven, harmful methods. The Conversation. [online] Available at: https://theconversation.com/students-are-not-hard-wired-to-learn-in-different-ways-we-need-to-stop-using-unproven-harmful-methods-63715.

Dunning, D., Johnson, K., Ehrlinger, J. and Kruger, J., 2003. Why people fail to recognize their own incompetence. *Current Directions in Psychological Science*, *12*(3), pp. 83–7.

Hattie, J., 2008. *Visible Learning: A Synthesis of Over 800 Meta-Analyses Relating to Achievement.* Abingdon: Routledge.

Kellogg, R.T., 2006. Professional writing expertise. *The Cambridge Handbook of Expertise and Expert Performance.* Cambridge: Cambridge University Press. pp. 389–402.

Pashler, H., McDaniel, M., Rohrer, D. and Bjork, R., 2008. Learning styles concepts and evidence. *Psychological Science in the Public Interest*, *9*(3), pp. 105–19.

Rosenshine, B., 2012. Principles of instruction: research-based strategies that all teachers should know. *American Educator*, *36*(1), p. 12.

Sadler, D.R., 2009. Indeterminacy in the use of preset criteria for assessment and grading. *Assessment & Evaluation in Higher Education*, *34*(2), pp. 159–79.

Simms, V., 2016. Mathematical mindsets: unleashing students' potential through creative math, inspiring messages and innovative teaching. *Research in Mathematics Education*, *18* (3), pp. 317–20.

Weale, S., 2016. Mental health champion for UK schools axed after criticising government. *The Guardian*, 4 May. [online] Available at: www.theguardian.com/education/2016/may/04/mental-health-champion-uk-schools-axed-after-criticising-government-natasha-devon.

Wiliam, D., 2011. *Embedded Formative Assessment*. Bloomington, IN: Solution Tree Press.

9

USING TECHNOLOGY

Key Points

This chapter will:

- Explore the various reasons for integrating different forms of technology into teaching
- Discuss how innovations spread and what this tends to look like in education
- Propose two questions to ask when considering the introduction of a new technology
- Look at the research related to the use of technology
- Ask what the use of a new technology will cause students to think about
- Ask what role artificial intelligence may play in education in the future
- Discuss the problem of obsolescence

Turtles

As ever in teaching, it is important to be clear about the objectives when introducing technology into the classroom. Broadly speaking, there are two: the objective for students to learn *about* technology, including how to use or programme different pieces of equipment, and the objective of using technology to *enhance* the learning of other knowledge, concepts or skills. Sometimes, these objectives may be conflated. For instance, we may ask students to use technology to produce a presentation about certain subject matter with a view to improving their technical skills in the process, or we might have a technical objective but hope that this also leads to an improvement in students' general reasoning abilities.

The aim of learning *about* technology is haunted by the ghosts of technologies past; the obsolescence that new gadgets suffer from. In the 1980s, I learnt how to use a word-processing package for the BBC Microcomputer, including the conventions required for naming files and the commands needed to justify text. A 1980s physics teacher looking for an application of electromagnetism to introduce to students may have chosen the tape recorder.

This latter example also demonstrates another problem with learning about technology; applications and innovations often blend concepts from quite different areas of knowledge. In the case of tape recorders, this would include materials science, sound, electromagnetism and more. Yet if we wish to build robust schemas of concepts in students' minds, it may be better to use a hierarchical approach. Applications certainly have a role in learning about any content area because they help to make ideas concrete, but drawing on applications always involves glossing over some of the key principles. You can't really deepen conceptual knowledge through applications alone and so they are not the best choice for building a conceptual course around. Technical training in specific skills is a different matter.

What about when the aims of learning *about* and *through* technology are complementary, for instance in a one-to-one laptop program that is intended to both enhance the learning of concepts and build students' Information and Communication Technology (ICT) skills? The colossus of Seymour Papert stands astride any such discussion, along with his programming language, LOGO, and his theory of 'constructionism'; a theory that is not to be confused with constructivism, even though they are similar.

You may be forgiven for thinking that Papert's aim was simply to teach computer programming. After all, he encouraged the practice of asking children to investigate the use of LOGO to draw shapes on a computer screen. Often, as in my own experience as a child, these shapes would be drawn out on a large piece of paper on the floor by a small pen-wielding robot dubbed a 'turtle'.

Yet Papert's goals were vaulting: 'The child programs the computer. And in teaching the computer how to think, children embark on an exploration about how they themselves think'. He believed that computers could be used to push children through the stages of development theorised by Jean Piaget (Papert, 1980), a theory that is no longer considered current by cognitive scientists (Willingham, 2008).

Unfortunately, the initial promise of LOGO was not realised. Students who spent considerable time – more than 50 hours – investigating the LOGO environment did indeed learn to produce short programs. However, their understanding was superficial and they tended to develop misconceptions (Mayer, 2004). We now know that this is typical of discovery learning environments for the reasons we have examined in previous chapters.

Cycles of innovation

There is an interesting literature that seeks to analyse how innovations spread. A popular model is Rogers's Diffusion Theory. It divides adopters of a new technology into categories according to the point when they engage: innovators, early adopters, early majority, late majority and laggards (Rogers, 1962). Although Rogers' own approach to diffusion is nuanced, a surface reading of his model implies that innovation is necessarily a good thing and all that we need to focus on is overcoming the resistance of laggards.

To help businesses better understand when to invest in new technologies, Gartner Inc., an American information technology research and advisory company, introduced the 'hype cycle' (Linden and Fenn, 2003). This is a little more pessimistic and suggests that expectations for new innovations are often inflated in the early stages of diffusion. Reminiscent of a journey in a Tolkien epic, the Gartner cycle passes through five key stages: the technology trigger, the peak of inflated expectations, the trough of disillusionment, the slope of enlightenment and finally the plateau of productivity. There's hype but there's also hope.

Perhaps more cynically, historian of education Larry Cuban has noticed three periods in the application of a new technology to the classroom, periods that may seem eerily familiar to experienced teachers. First, extravagant claims are made for the new technology. Second, academic studies show limited or unimaginative use by teachers. Finally, teachers are blamed for the lack of successful implementation rather than those who made the initial claims (Cuban and Jandric, 2015).

What Cuban's model serves to illustrate is that the effective use of technology is not an inevitability. It is not an unqualified good that we can simply heap upon education.

Television

In 1967, Richard E. Clark left the television industry to pursue a doctorate in education, 'based in large part on a belief that television could revolutionize education' (Robinson and Bligh, 2016). Over the coming years, Clark grew frustrated. He noticed a conflict between some of the evidence presented in his psychology classes and the claims made by educational technology instructors. He started to ask questions of these instructors and query conclusions that he perceived to lack empirical support.

Later in his career, Clark accepted a request to review the key evidence in the field. In examining carefully controlled studies, he found no learning benefits associated with the use of *any* particular medium, be it teachers, books, radio or television. The effects were all about the same. And yet other researchers were finding quite large effects in favour of newer media. How could this be reconciled?

Clark's insight was to notice that the studies that demonstrated no effect for the new media were studies in which the same teachers designed *both* the materials used in the new media *and* the teaching that took place in the comparison condition. What initially seemed like an effect of new media was in fact an effect of different people designing the teaching (Robinson and Bligh, 2016).

This gives us a good reason to pause and consider education research more generally. A fundamental principle of science is that we vary only one factor at a time. However, it is often difficult in education to determine what 'one factor' is. If we wish to look at the effect of the medium of teaching – a live teacher versus a television, for instance – then the key is to vary *only this factor* and nothing else. It is possible to use the gold-standard method of a randomised controlled trial (Torgerson and Torgerson, 2001) and yet still generate spurious results if we are relaxed about the 'controlled' component and test a whole combination of factors at a time. This occurs far too often in education research and is one of the reasons why I always start reading an academic paper at the 'methods' section. There is usually no subterfuge at play, it is simply very difficult to vary just one thing when we are looking at an intervention as broad as an educational approach.

Two key questions

Given that the positive effects of technology are not guaranteed, how can teachers evaluate the potential of a new technology? I suggest we need to ask two key questions:

1. What are students intended to learn through the adoption of this technology? If it is something timeless such as 'how to solve linear equations' then it will not matter as much if the technology itself is transient, although you will want to be able to invest in it for at least a few years. If the intended learning is about the technology then you will need to be convinced that the technology itself, or at least the key principles – such as programming – have a decent future. If the objectives are vague or cut across a range of different categories, then this should give us reason to hesitate and ask the second question.
2. What is the evidence that this technology will lead to improved outcomes in the intended learning when compared to existing approaches that do not make use of this technology? In this case, we should look for high-quality, peer-reviewed studies and be cautious of hype put about by public relations firms. Sometimes, the answer will be obvious: if the intended learning is about spreadsheets then you need a computer, a pen and paper will not do. However, you may find yourself weighing different technology options against each other.

These questions are based on the assumption that we wish to maximise the effectiveness of the teaching that utilises the new technology. We may plausibly have a different objective, such as offering a variety of activities for motivational reasons. In this case, a rigorous effectiveness test would not be necessary.

Throwing it at the wall and seeing what sticks

A number of programmes have been constructed on the premise that simply increasing access to technology by supplying more of it to schools will lead to improvements in learning. For instance, schools may adopt a one-to-one laptop or tablet programme. Twenty years ago, this may have looked more like installing computer laboratories in schools.

The evidence suggests that this is not a great investment. A group of academics from the National Bureau of Economic Research in the United States set about trying to analyse the data from rigorous studies that assessed the effect of providing more access to computers and related technologies (e.g. fast broadband). Few studies actually met their selection criteria. Of those that did, there was generally a lack of any significant effect, although there were hints that such programmes might help improve the computer skills of some disadvantaged groups, as well as hints of some potentially negative effects. Interestingly, given the previous discussion of television and other media, less rigorous studies were more likely to appear to demonstrate a positive effect (Escueta et al., 2017). Given the cost of such programmes, this does not make a compelling case.

The effect of access to computers has also been investigated as part of the international PISA and TIMSS studies of student achievement. These use survey questions to try to determine the frequency of student computer use in lessons. Once socioeconomic status is taken into account, these studies tend to show either no relationship or a potentially negative relationship, i.e. more computer use is associated with worse levels of achievement (Kadijevich, 2015; Zhang and Liu, 2016; Petko et al., 2017).

It might, at this stage, be worth asking the question: what did we expect? Technology may possess the cute charm of a neophyte, but when we examine these studies then it is clear that we are assessing the value of something pretty general. What, for instance, would we predict to be the effect of increasing the number of books in a school or of lengthening the opening hours of the school library? What would we predict to happen if we gave schools lots of televisions or video projectors? A reasonable person might suggest that it depends on what the books are, what the library is like and what is shown on the televisions or video projectors.

This is where a study conducted at West Point military academy in the United States might be able to help. Researchers ran a randomised controlled trial (RCT), splitting economics students into three groups. One group was banned from using computers in class. A second group was free to use them. The third and final group was allowed to use computers but in such a way that screens could be viewed by instructors, thus limiting the scope for students to be checking emails, Facebook and so on (Carter et al., 2017).

The results showed that students in the group where computers were banned performed significantly better than students in either of the two groups where computers were allowed. This suggests that it is not simply the ability of computers to distract us that may be detrimental. One plausible hypothesis is that students who used laptops to take notes in class were basically writing down everything they heard with little thought, whereas students who had a pen and paper necessarily had to process the information in some way in order to take handwritten notes. It was that processing that gave the learning benefit.

Both the distraction hypothesis and the note-taking hypothesis are consistent with the model of the mind outlined in Chapter 3. In order for biologically secondary knowledge to pass into the long-term memory, it must be processed in working memory. If working memory is engaged in a different task, or if it is not really engaged in any processing at all, then there is no mechanism by which learning can take place. Daniel Willingham puts this succinctly as 'memory is the residue of thought' (Willingham, 2009).

Software solutions

There is a significant market in software or 'apps' that aim to address learning needs. One area that shows promise is the enhancement of maths learning. Reviews of the evidence regularly suggest that some kinds of adaptive maths software – programmes that alter the next question a student is asked depending on their response to the previous one – have positive effects on learning (Escueta et al., 2017). One package that was subjected to a randomised controlled trial encouraged parents to interact with their children around a bedtime story and related maths problem. Children assigned to receive the intervention showed gains in their mathematical ability when compared to students assigned to a similar intervention that lacked the maths problems (Berkowitz et al., 2015).

One obvious use of software is for 'gamification'. Computer games are addictive and young people seem to be able to immerse themselves in these games for hours. This is in stark contrast to the level of attention that many students are able to maintain for academic work. Yet computer games are also a learning environment. Players have to learn how to defeat the bad guys or solve the puzzle. Can we therefore use computer games as a way of teaching academic content in a manner that is pleasurable and engaging for our students?

A US study investigated the potential for narrative games and points to some key issues to consider. In a series of experiments, college students were randomly assigned to either play an adventure game with the aim of learning scientific knowledge about pathogens or to sit through a slide show on the same content. In a later test, students who played the game actually performed worse than students who saw the slide show. Removing the narrative element of the game made little difference (Adams et al., 2012).

Again, I think it is important to return to our model of the mind. Students engaging with adaptive maths software will be primarily thinking about mathematics. Playing a game will take students away from the intended focus if the narrative or gameplay element is not intrinsic to what needs to be learnt. For instance, a quiz game will focus mainly on the questions but a narrative game may have an overarching story that only loosely relates to the objectives. Students may expend more mental resources thinking about the narrative than the content to be learnt. If you then compare this with a relatively modest form of explicit teaching, you may find explicit teaching is superior because it focuses students more on the content. It all depends on what we are comparing.

For instance, if we return to the example of the bedtime story software, *any* immersion in mathematics content is a bonus. In this case, the alternative to engaging with the maths software is not to watch a slide show but to complete no mathematics.

I recall Dr Jan Plass of New York University discussing this issue when visiting Australia. Plass has worked on optimising the design of learning games and he addressed research such as the kind that I have just described on narrative games. His point was that, without games, some of the students he worked with would not be engaged in education *at all*. These were not highly motivated college students who would otherwise be prepared to sit through a slide show.

So it is hard to consider the role of games without bearing in mind the discussion about motivation from Chapter 4. Ideally, the game element will be enjoyable enough that students will persist until they start having some success with the intended learning. This should then feed forward into greater self-efficacy. Over time, as students become more motivated by the content, the need to dress it up as a game may fade. This is highly plausible as a way to get students back on the learning bus but testing such a hypothesis is difficult.

One review of the field of game-based learning found some gains for learning in physical education – particularly so-called 'exergames' that mix gaming with exercise – history and languages but little evidence of a positive impact in science and mathematics. The researchers also recommended stripping out research on gaming from that on simulations because these could work in different ways (Young et al., 2012).

Simulations have the potential to be extremely powerful in subjects such as science (Rutten et al., 2012) because they allow us to conduct experiments that are hard to do in real life or visualise things that are hard to see, such as the particles in a gas. They also have the advantage of being visual and so we are able to process them simultaneously with a verbal explanation (Mayer, 2017).

Incidentally

One of the effects of dumping tech into classrooms is that teachers feel obliged to use it in an incidental way. For instance, a history teacher may wish to teach students some key facts about the Renaissance and how the Renaissance changed Europe. Observing that the students have all brought a laptop to class under the school's one-to-one device policy, the teacher may ask them to make a PowerPoint presentation that demonstrates an understanding of these objectives.

Again, if we return to our model of the mind, we should ask what this task will require students to think about. Will their minds spend time in the Renaissance or will they be thinking about animations and searching for clip art? Whenever I have set such a task I have been impressed by the surface features of the finished product but dissatisfied with the level of content knowledge and understanding that it displays. If our objective is to teach certain ICT skills then we need to be explicit about that, but if we think we can address them incidentally and have no negative effect on academic learning then we are mistaken.

This is exactly the same case as the one that applies to more low-tech tasks such as poster work or preparing an oral presentation.

We are the robots

At the time of writing, there is a great deal of hype around artificial intelligence (AI). Claims are made about the potential for AI to disrupt the world of business and educators worry about the future for their students. Are we preparing them for the coming world or are we training them for jobs that will be replaced by AI?

The role of AI in the classroom is less clear. Ultimately, we may have intelligent tutoring systems or roboteachers that will displace flesh-and-bone teachers entirely. If this is our ultimate fate then it is still a long way off. However, an area where AI is already encroaching on the work of teachers is in assessment.

At the time of writing, the Australian Curriculum, Assessment and Reporting Authority (ACARA) is about to embark upon a trial of using computers to mark responses to the NAPLAN writing paper taken by all Australian students in Years 3, 5, 7 and 9. Initially, they intend to have each script marked by both a human and a computer. If the results are satisfactory, the hope is to move to a greater role for computer marking in future (Schwartz, 2017).

On the surface, the use of AI to assess writing is a great idea. Marking writing is time-consuming for teachers and AI could reduce the burden, allowing teachers to focus on more important aspects of the work. The is some evidence that an AI focus on the technical aspects of writing frees teachers to provide higher-level feedback (Wilson and Czik, 2016).

The main problem with automated writing assessment is an almost philosophical one. We write in order to convey meaning to another person and yet a computer fundamentally does not understand that meaning.

There are a number of ways that automated systems work, based upon principles of machine learning. Computers may be fed a database of papers already graded by teachers at different levels. They may be given a list of rules for good writing. Some software will even attempt to address meaning by looking for key content-related words and the way that they are being used. In this case, relevant data will need to be uploaded into the computer's database (Hoang and Kunnan, 2016).

The field is advancing all the time. Yet even if we do manage to develop highly reliable systems for grading writing, it is not clear that the issue of meaning will be resolved. For instance, certain quantifiable aspects of a piece of writing – e.g. the number of words written (Perelman, 2014) – may well be good proxies for quality writing *at the moment*, but as soon as people realise what the machine is looking for there will be a temptation to give it what it wants, especially if the stakes are high. The grades we generate will now be less valid. The fear is that we will incentivise students to write wordy responses that contain a certain number of compound sentences, liberal use of the word 'but', and so on while paying only a passing interest in addressing the writing prompt. This is identical to the argument about the validity of rubrics that we visited in Chapter 4.

Ultimately, the skill of good writing is to convey meaning with clarity, precision and concision. Until computers can evaluate meaning, it seems unlikely that they will eliminate the need for humans.

Obsolescence

There are those who argue that the rate at which knowledge is currently increasing means that the old idea of a textbook is outdated (e.g. Arbesman, 2012). By the time students finish a course, it is claimed, the content of their textbook will have been superseded. This may be true but it will depend upon what course they are studying. A key principle that we should bear in mind is that knowledge *does* become obsolete but it is often the *most recent* knowledge that becomes obsolete first. Consider the following list of items that could plausibly be taught in school:

1. How to use the 'Inverse Normal' function on a TI-Nspire™ calculator
2. Like poles repel, unlike poles attract
3. William Shakespeare used classical allusions in writing his plays
4. Volcanoes are ruptures in the Earth's crust that allow hot lava to escape to the surface from a magma chamber below
5. Captain James Cook discovered Australia
6. Anadiplosis is a rhetorical technique where the last word of a sentence is repeated as the first word of the next sentence
7. There are risks associated with posting personal content to MySpace
8. There are nine planets in the solar system

The first item will be out-of-date when the TI-Nspire™ calculator is superseded, although its successor may work in a similar way. We could argue that item 5 is obsolete because many Australians would now wish to emphasise that the country was inhabited before Europeans arrived and so it wasn't really 'discovered' by Cook. Item 7 is specific to a social media platform – MySpace – that is no longer popular and yet the general principle still stands when we apply it to other platforms. Item 8 is no longer true because we recently changed the definition of a planet to exclude Pluto (although it has not gone away).

The rest of the items are pretty timeless. They may represent incomplete and simplistic analyses but it is unlikely that these will be found to be mistaken in the foreseeable future. And that is the case for many of the more fundamental curriculum objectives that we teach in schools. A lot of the media discussion seems to imply that ideas go out of date because we discover that they were wrong all along. The reality is more complex. Ideas may change due to changing technology or new or more complete interpretations. The implication is that we risk little by teaching knowledge as it currently stands.

When I first started teaching physics, I was required to teach students the three possible fates of the universe, depending on its mass: a big crunch, a continual, slowing expansion and a boundary state between the two. Since this time, we have discovered dark energy and the idea that the expansion of the universe may be speeding up. This is the clearest example that I can recall of something that was factually wrong. And yet any student who was taught the original model will easily be able to accommodate the new one because all of the models rest upon a conceptual understanding of gravity.

Conclusions

Technology is not a set of magic beans that we may plant in order to grow a beanstalk of learning. However, if we approach it with the right attitude, technology can offer benefits. When examining whether to introduce technology, we need be clear about what we intend our students to learn as a result and we also need to be clear that there is evidence to show that the technology we are considering will boost that learning. We have to bear in mind that technology is potentially distracting and can cause students to think about a whole range of factors outside of the intended learning and it may have unintended consequences for tasks such as taking notes. New technologies such as artificial intelligence have the potential to completely transform the teaching profession, although this probably won't happen soon.

References

Adams, D.M., Mayer, R.E., MacNamara, A., Koenig, A. and Wainess, R., 2012. Narrative games for learning: testing the discovery and narrative hypotheses. *Journal of Educational Psychology*, *104*(1), p. 235.

Arbesman, A., 2012. Be forewarned: your knowledge is decaying. *Harvard Business Review*, 5 November. [online] Available at: https://hbr.org/2012/11/be-forewarned-your-knowledge-i.

Berkowitz, T., Schaeffer, M.W., Maloney, E.A., Peterson, L., Gregor, C., Levine, S.C. and Beilock, S.L., 2015. Math at home adds up to achievement in school. *Science*, *350*(6257), pp. 196–8.

Carter, S.P., Greenberg, K. and Walker, M.S., 2017. The impact of computer usage on academic performance: evidence from a randomized trial at the United States Military Academy. *Economics of Education Review*, *56*, pp. 118–32.

Cuban, L. and Jandrić, P., 2015. The dubious promise of educational technologies: historical patterns and future challenges. *E-Learning and Digital Media*, *12*(3–4), pp. 425–39.

Escueta, M., Quan, V., Nickow, A.J. and Oreopoulos, P., 2017. *Education Technology: An Evidence-Based Review*. No. w23744. Cambridge, MA: National Bureau of Economic Research.

Hoang, G.T.L. and Kunnan, A.J., 2016. Automated essay evaluation for English language learners: a case study of *MY Access*. *Language Assessment Quarterly*, *13*(4), pp. 359–76.

Kadijevich, D.M., 2015. A dataset from TIMSS to examine the relationship between computer use and mathematics achievement. *British Journal of Educational Technology*, *46*(5), pp. 984–7.

Linden, A. and Fenn, J., 2003. Understanding Gartner's hype cycles. *Strategic Analysis Report*, N° R-20-1971. Stanford, CT: Gartner, Inc.

Mayer, R.E., 2004. Should there be a three-strikes rule against pure discovery learning? *American Psychologist*, *59*(1), p. 14.

Mayer, R.E., 2017. Using multimedia for e-learning. *Journal of Computer Assisted Learning*, 13 June. DOI: 10.1111/jcal.12197.

Papert, S., 1980. *Mindstorms: Children, Computers, and Powerful Ideas*. New York: Basic Books, Inc.

Perelman, L., 2014. When 'the state of the art' is counting words. *Assessing Writing*, *21*, pp. 104–11.

Petko, D., Cantieni, A. and Prasse, D., 2017. Perceived quality of educational technology matters: a secondary analysis of students' ICT use, ICT-related attitudes, and PISA 2012 test scores. *Journal of Educational Computing Research*, *54*(8), pp. 1070–91.

Robinson, D.H. and Bligh, R.A., 2016. An interview with Richard E. Clark. *Educational Psychology Review*, *28*(4), pp. 875–91.

Rogers, E.M. 1962. *Diffusion of Innovations*. New York: Free Press.

Rutten, N., Van Joolingen, W.R. and Van der Veen, J.T., 2012. The learning effects of computer simulations in science education. *Computers & Education*, *58*(1), pp. 136–53.

Schwartz, S., 2017. Of course teachers fear robo-marking. *Daily Telegraph*, 19 October. [online] Available at: www.dailytelegraph.com.au/rendez view/of-course-teachers-fear-robomarking/news-story/6c3af82b43d5cf1 3183e231ae0b65e3f

Torgerson, C.J. and Torgerson, D.J., 2001. The need for randomised controlled trials in educational research. *British Journal of Educational Studies*, *49*(3), pp. 316–28.

Willingham, D.T., 2008. What is developmentally appropriate practice? *American Educator*, *32*(2), p. 34.

Willingham, D.T., 2009. *Why Don't Students Like School?: A Cognitive Scientist Answers Questions about How the Mind Works and What It Means for the Classroom*. San Francisco: Jossey-Bass.

Wilson, J. and Czik, A., 2016. Automated essay evaluation software in English Language Arts classrooms: effects on teacher feedback, student motivation, and writing quality. *Computers & Education*, *100*, pp. 94–109.

Young, M.F., Slota, S., Cutter, A.B., Jalette, G., Mullin, G., Lai, B., Simeoni, Z., Tran, M. and Yukhymenko, M., 2012. Our princess is in another castle: a review of trends in serious gaming for education. *Review of Educational Research*, *82*(1), pp. 61–89.

Zhang, D. and Liu, L., 2016. How does ICT use influence students' achievements in math and science over time? Evidence from PISA 2000 to 2012. *Eurasia Journal of Mathematics, Science & Technology Education*, *12*(9), pp. 2431–49.

10

THE PHONICS DEBATE

Key Points

This chapter will:

- Discuss the origins of writing and whether these origins support the idea of students naturally acquiring reading ability
- Explain that the particular challenges of the English language make learning to read difficult
- Outline some of the evidence supporting systematic synthetic phonics
- Describe the battles that have raged around methods of teaching reading and suggest some reasons for their persistence
- Draw out some lessons that might relate to the education debate more generally

Ancient clay tablets

We don't know how long humans have been speaking to each other. Modern humans evolved over a quarter of a million years ago (Sample, 2017) and may have been talking to each other even before that. We can imagine a slow, gradual process whereby the kinds of calls and signals that are common in other animals evolved into the abstract language that we possess today.

In contrast, we can be clearer about the origin of writing. It probably appeared for the first time around 5000 years ago in Mesopotamia. We have an interesting record of its development left by the ancient Sumerians. First, we find small clay tokens that perhaps represent a way of counting goods such as grain or cattle. Then we find these tokens sealed in round clay envelopes, perhaps to avoid tampering. Next we see marks made on the outside of the envelopes that resemble the tokens held inside. Finally, someone must have realised that once there were markings on the outside, there was no need to keep the tokens on the inside and so the system became one of simple clay marks made with a stylus. This writing became known as 'cuneiform' meaning 'wedge-shaped' after the appearance of these markings (Postgate, 1992).

Writing seems to have begun as a concrete way of recording transactions, far from its current literary and intellectual role. That role evolved over many years and the course of this development was not obvious to those who took part in it. We may, with the benefit of hindsight, think those clay envelopes a little unnecessary, yet the scribes who made them took them seriously.

The first writing was pictographic, with tokens representing the items they were intended to denote. Pictographic systems grew in complexity and, over time, grew to represent the sounds in words. Some of these derivatives used symbols to represent syllables. Over a thousand years passed before the emergence of alphabetic languages with symbols intended to denote separate sounds (Millard, 1986). Initially, these letters only represented consonants, with vowels being added later.

The shift from symbolic writing to writing that somehow attempts to encode the sounds of words is important. The evidence suggests that a system where a different symbol is used to represent each word would place a limit on the number of words that people would be able to learn to read and write, a limit far below the number of words used in most modern languages. Even languages such as Chinese, that are often thought to have a separate character for each word, actually make use of sound-cuing systems supplemented by symbols that help classify the word into categories (McGuinness, 2006).

It is important to emphasise two aspects of the story of writing. First, the origins of speech and of writing are separated by vast amounts of time. Even once writing had been invented, it was only a small class of scribes who knew its secrets, with mass literacy arriving in developed countries as late as the 19th century. Second, there was nothing inevitable about the development of writing or the form that it would eventually take, particularly from the perspective of those involved in developing it. Taken together, these aspects inform us that speaking and writing are quite different processes. And that's important for our ideas about how to teach literacy.

Naturalism

As we saw in Chapter 3, we can consider the knowledge that humans accumulate as belonging to two broad categories: biologically primary and biologically secondary knowledge. The first kind is something that we see children acquire across all cultures and without specific efforts made to teach it. This is possible because it is knowledge that we have evolved to acquire.

However, biologically secondary knowledge is knowledge that has been created by culture and that is therefore not something that we have evolved to acquire. Given that writing has been around for only a few thousand years and, for much of that time, it was the preserve of a few, we cannot have evolved a mental module for learning to read and write. Instead, we need to co-opt mental functions that have evolved for other purposes and this is why learning to read and write takes effort.

Unfortunately, the progressive educational philosophy that grew to prominence from the mid-19th century, and that is still in many ways current, suggests that *all* learning should be natural (Egan, 2004). If learning is hard and children don't always enjoy it, then this is a sign that there is something wrong with the way we are teaching. This view is based upon a category error; to insist, as whole language advocates

Kenneth and Yetta Goodman do (Goodman and Goodman, 1976), that 'acquisition of literacy is an extension of natural language learning for all children. Instruction which is consistent with this understanding facilitates learning. Instruction which does not build on the process of natural language learning will, in some respects, be at cross purposes with learners' natural tendencies', is to commit the mistake of assuming that learning to read and write is like learning to listen to, and speak, a language. They are not the same, but this assumption is a philosophical stance rather than one based upon evidence and so is resistant to challenge.

An opaque orthography

The set of rules governing the ways that a modern written language maps to spoken sounds is known as its 'orthography', after the Greek words for 'correct' and 'writing'. We can think of the act of converting written letters into real or imagined sounds as an act of 'decoding'. Some languages make this straightforward by having a transparent orthography; this means each letter or letter combination represents a discrete sound with no ambiguity. Finnish is an example of such a language. Learning a language with a transparent orthography is relatively simple because, once you have committed the various letter–sound relationships to memory, decoding words is straightforward and you may instead focus on meaning. Many European countries lack methods for assessing simple decoding because it is so simple that virtually all children pick it up with ease (McGuinness, 2006).

English isn't like that. It is rather more opaque. There *are* letter–sound relationships but there are also a lot of exceptions and alternatives, making English devilish to learn. And it works in both directions; the same sound can have different spellings – e.g. the 'oo' sound in 'boot' and 'flute' – and the same spelling can represent different sounds – think of the sound made by the letters 'ou' in 'soup', 'clout' and 'mourn'.

Much of the complexity of English stems from its very vibrancy; its tendency to adopt words from other languages. I remember a head-teacher I once worked for who insisted on pronouncing 'questionnaire' as something approximating 'kestionair', illustrating the bind we find ourselves in when presented with loan words – should we use the original pronunciation or an anglicised one? In this case, much of the amusement stemmed from the fact that all of the other members of her leadership team started to do the same. And how do you say 'pain au chocolat'? I've found this particular noun phrase so confounding over the years that I now generally gesture, nod and say, 'Can I have one of those please? Thanks.'

The opaque orthography of English leads to an understandable dilemma about how to teach it. Should we attempt to teach the letter–sound relationships with all of their variations and deviations – i.e. a phonics approach – or should we try some other method? This is a debate that has raged for a long time and is not resolved even now.

It is easy to find lucid and often quite convincing arguments that suggest that teaching phonics is a Sisyphean task. For instance, Stephen Krashen has argued that learning the rules of English is futile because there are so many exceptions (Krashen, 2002). Another tack is to suggest that according to English rules of pronunciation, the word 'fish' could be spelled as 'ghoti'. The 'gh' would be pronounced as in the word 'enough', the 'o' as in 'women' and the 'ti' as in 'action'. This is often attributed to George Bernard Shaw but according to research by Charles Robinson, a professor of English in the United States, the idea dates to 1855 and originated with William Ollier, the son of the publisher Charles Ollier (Zimmer, 2010). Ingenious though William may have been, there is an error in the reasoning that somewhat overstates the opacity of English.

Single letters or groups of letters that represent a single sound are known as 'graphemes' and the sounds they represent are 'phonemes'. Crucially, in English, the letters alone are not enough to determine the phoneme because this also depends upon the position of the grapheme in a word. So the grapheme 'gh' would never make an 'f' sound at the start of a word, only at the end. This makes the rules of English more complex than languages with a transparent orthography but it also indicates that the relationships between graphemes and phonemes are not as random as we might at first imagine.

Once we take into account that many English words originate in other languages and the rules are often consistent within those groups of words, we can recognise even more order. If you ever watch a high-level spelling bee competition, you will notice that the contestants often ask for the language of origin of each word (I once saw this demonstrated by Mandy Nayton, Executive Officer of The Dyslexia–SPELD Foundation in Australia).

Still, it is reasonable to suggest that things are more complicated than they need to be. If we want to avoid teaching lots of rules – the grapheme–phoneme relationships and rules about word positions and so on – then we need to have a viable alternative. English orthography may be unnecessarily complex but if children don't learn it then what do they learn instead? Do we expect them to simply memorise whole words? That doesn't seem viable. To misquote Churchill, perhaps phonics is the worst way of teaching reading, apart from all of the others.

We now have solid evidence for phonics from no less than three reports commissioned by English-speaking countries (National Reading Panel, 2000 [United States]; Rowe, 2005 [Australia]; Rose, 2006 [UK]). What is more, we even have evidence about which types of phonics teaching work best.

Synthetic phonics programmes teach the relationships between individual phonemes and the graphemes that represent them, such as the relationship between the relevant sound and the 'oo' grapheme. Teachers using these programmes then ask children to 'blend' these phonemes together to form a whole word when reading – this is the assembly or 'synthesis' that gives rise to the term 'synthetic'. For instance, in decoding the word 'book' they would notice three graphemes; 'b', 'oo' and 'k'. Putting these together in sequence would allow them to pronounce the word. If the child also holds a concept of what a 'book' is then he or she will understand the writer's intended meaning.

Conversely, 'analytic' phonics programmes take a different approach. They start with the whole word and teachers draw the attention of students to similarities in particular sounds. For instance, a teacher might write a number of words that start with the same letter and ask students to notice what sound this makes.

'Systematic' synthetic phonics are those that proceed in a structured way in which each new grapheme–phoneme relationship is introduced one at a time. For instance, the grapheme 'oo' commonly represents two sounds so students may first learn just the one relationship. This means that reading materials need to be closely aligned with the particular relationships that a child has learnt.

The available evidence suggests that systematic synthetic phonics is generally superior to other approaches to teaching phonics knowledge (National Research Council, 1998; Rowe, 2005).

Yet there is little that is more rancorous than a discussion of phonics in education. Children's authors such as Mem Fox and Michael Rosen regularly express their scepticism of approaches to phonics teaching. For instance, Rosen suggests that correctly sounding out the words in a sentence or paragraph is not 'reading' because his definition of reading includes an understanding of what the words mean (Rosen, 2017). The education blogger Andrew Old has dubbed this the fear of 'Ron Burgundy Syndrome', after the fictional protagonist of the film *Anchorman* who displays an ability to read from an autocue without ever seemingly processing what the words mean (Old, 2017).

Fox shares Rosen's view that reading is all about 'making meaning' rather than deriving sounds from the words we see on a page. She gives the example of the word 'tear' that could be pronounced in two different ways and mean two different things depending on the sentence it is in. To Fox, this highlights the importance of context in reading. Fox thinks that most children will learn to read whatever the method and so greater importance should be placed on issues of meaning (Fox, 2008).

Clearly, in the example of the word 'tear', context *is* important. But so is decoding. If the child cannot decode the word then he or she is reduced to guessing. For instance, if the word appears in the sentence, 'Jasmine decided to tear the page in two', and is accompanied by a picture of a child holding a piece of paper, a reader without phonics knowledge might conclude that 'tear' should be read as 'fold'. A reader *with* phonics knowledge will be left with two options, one of which doesn't makes sense, even without the picture, and so will correctly decode the word.

I don't think any advocate of systematic synthetic phonics would argue that merely turning words into sounds is sufficient, but they may suggest that it is necessary. Many such advocates subscribe to the 'simple view of reading', which suggests that reading ability is the sum of two other abilities; the ability to turn words into sounds and the ability to comprehend what these sounds mean (Hoover and Gough, 1990). Although dubbed 'simple', the consequences are far from straightforward. The ability to comprehend what words *mean* is a biologically primary process that involves our evolved speaking and listening abilities whereas the ability to decode written words is biologically secondary and therefore effortful to learn.

Moreover, oral comprehension races ahead of reading ability for young children and so it is important for parents and schools to introduce them to important vocabulary, general knowledge and key principles that they will later draw upon when reading more complex texts. Relying only on texts that children are able to read will result in students not making gains in oral comprehension that they are capable of making (Biemiller, 2003). An insistence on reading as 'meaning making' misunderstands that there are two components to reading that have to work together and neither of which can be neglected.

Why is there still disagreement? Why does phonics create so much sound and fury?

War

The passions that fuel the phonics debate can be traced to ideas current in the 19th century that grew to prominence by the start of the 20th century. Education reformers of that era often believed that classrooms were unnatural and they were concerned about the idea of drilling students in meaningless facts. One set of meaningless facts that stood out from the rest were the letter–sound relationships that were taught as part of the rudimentary phonics instruction of the time.

As far back as 1841, Horace Mann complained that the letters of the alphabet are 'skeleton-shaped, bloodless, ghostly apparitions, and hence it is no wonder that the children look and feel so death-like, when compelled to face them' (Association of Masters of the Boston Public Schools, 1844). When convinced of such a position, there are two rational responses. The first is to object to literacy as a goal of education and some reformers were indeed ambivalent to reading, viewing it as unnecessary for living a great life. Instead, they valorised the relative advantages of obtaining practical knowledge. The second response is to accept that reading is a valid objective of education, but that it should proceed from the whole-word or even whole-sentence level as this would be more natural and motivating. Many reformers adopted this line (Ravitch, 2001).

Teachers generally work alone with groups of students and so it can be hard to determine exactly what approach is typical. It seems likely that teachers hold on to practices that they have found to be successful, long after experts have starting advocating for an alternative, an effect that will always confound attempts to be definitive about how reading is being taught at any given time. What *is* clear is that by the middle of the 20th century, the expert consensus had coalesced around a whole-word approach to reading (Ravitch, 2001; Kim, 2008).

Whole-word methods usually involved introducing students to a limited number of words at a time that they were expected to learn by sight. Texts became predictable and repetitive in an effort to ensure that students had repeated exposure to the targeted words. This took some of the shine off an approach that was intended to be more natural and motivating than the phonics drills it replaced (McGuinness, 2006).

Into this setting stepped Jeanne Chall, a key figure in the history of the debate about reading methods. Chall conducted reviews of the evidence in 1967, 1983, 1986, 1987 and 1992–3. With the caveat that our understanding of phonics has become more sophisticated over time, it is fair to say that each of these reviews found broadly the same thing: teacher-centred approaches that involve explicit teaching of phonics in a systematic way are more effective than whole-word methods, or innovative methods where phonics is taught incidentally or only when needed (Chall, 2000).

Despite suggestions to the contrary, none of Chall's findings pre-clude the introduction of good children's literature. The caricature of children endlessly rehearsing grapheme–phoneme relationships and never being read a story is more of a rhetorical device than an actual teaching method.

It is hard to contemplate the length of time and the volume of scholarly work that Chall devoted to repeatedly finding the same thing and not wonder whether this must have been a frustrating career. It was certainly a contentious one. Writing in the preface to Chall's 2000 book, Marilyn Jager Adams recalled Chall warning her that if she wrote the truth about phonics, she would 'make enemies'. Adams observed, 'as the evidence in favor of systematic, explicit phonics instruction for beginners increased, so too did the vehemence and nastiness of the backlash. The goal became one of discrediting not just the research, but the integrity and character of those who conducted it' (Chall, 2000).

Following Chall's pioneering work in the 1960s, whole-word approaches were forced to back-peddle until they eventually returned with force under the guise of the 'whole language' movement that became increasingly influential, even conventional, by the 1980s. Whole language attempted to address some of the problems of the previous whole-word approaches by elevating the role of children's literature in the process of learning to read. Reading was intended to be a natural and authentic process, rather than one where words were chopped up into component parts. The rhetoric around whole language was often strongly political, with Kenneth Goodman, a leading advocate, repeatedly attacking opponents for advancing the agenda of the 'far right' (Ravitch, 2001).

Despite the focus on authentic literature, whole-language teachers still often made use of texts with a predictable structure (Johnston, 2000). This is likely for pragmatic reasons. If students cannot sound out a word and they cannot predict it then how is reading meant to occur?

There is strong correlational evidence that mandating whole-language methods led to a decline in the reading ability of students. For instance, after adopting a whole-language literacy curriculum in 1987, California went on to record the worst reading scores of the entire United States (Turner et al., 1996).

Perhaps as a result of this negative evidence, over the years the debate has strayed from the original confines of a discussion about the most effective way to teach reading. Effectiveness research requires some testable outcomes. For instance, in order to decide whether Method A is better than Method B there needs to be a reading test that assesses reading ability after children are taught by these methods. If we reject the very possibility of such a test then we can reject the research evidence, even if we neglect to supplant it with a viable alternative.

And so there are those who argue that the social sciences are qualitatively different to the physical sciences. Trying to work out the effect of a reading programme on human children is far more complicated than trying to work out the effect of a nuclear reaction, the argument proceeds, because there are so many variables at play when it comes to humans. Humans experience the world subjectively – they have opinions, tastes, emotions – and it is not possible to predict exactly what will happen to a given person in a real-world situation due to a given intervention (Biesta, 2015). Therefore, the scientific method, if it even really exists, is not appropriate for the social sciences. We at least need to consider other kinds of research as equally valid. Insisting on evidence from scientific trials is naïve and likely to be labelled by critics as 'positivism' or 'scientism' (e.g. Cunningham, 2001; Biesta, 2009).

This argument falls down on a number of levels. First, it implies the existence of a method that, when applied to the social sciences, is superior to the scientific method. If I judge research methods against the objective of trying to find the best approach to teaching reading, mathematics or anything else, I can't find any that are superior to the scientific method; a method that includes the consideration of experimental and correlational data. And yet critics may argue that I have chosen the wrong objective. Many researchers, ambivalent to calls to improve the *effectiveness* of reading instruction, would instead seek to make it more democratic or critical or socially just. In turn, I would argue that to meet any of these objectives requires it to first be effective.

Second, the argument that humans are not predictable is moot. Nobody ever claimed that it is possible to predict the exact effect of an intervention on each individual. The point of the statistical methods used by researchers is that they look for an average effect across a group of subjects. If more children learn by Method A than Method B then that is worth knowing, even if some don't learn by Method A. We can then research this further.

In the case of phonics, the proposition that some subgroups would learn better through alternative means is one that lacks robust evidence. The 2006 Rose review conducted on behalf of the UK government cautioned that teaching alternative strategies for decoding words, such as using context or picture clues to make a prediction, is potentially harmful (Rose, 2006). Even those children who are able to implicitly derive letter–sound relationships without explicit teaching may benefit from having better spelling knowledge, and superior knowledge of phonics may even aid reading comprehension (Tunmer and Chapman, 2012).

Dead reckoning

Longitude is a measure of how far east or west an object is from a reference point on the globe. The problem of finding longitude at sea plagued 18th century seafarers and was considered so important by the British government that in 1714 they instituted a prize for anyone who could solve it. Finding latitude, the position north or south of the equator, was relatively easy from the elevation of the Sun, but up until this point, sailors had used a technique known as 'dead reckoning' for finding longitude. By throwing a knotted rope overboard they would estimate their speed and so attempt to work out how far they had travelled. It worked, but not very well and led to a number of disasters where ships foundered on rocks and sailors lost their lives.

After some moderately successful attempts to make use of the positions of astronomical objects to find a ship's longitude, the longitude problem was finally cracked by the introduction of clocks – 'chronometers' – that could keep accurate time at sea. This was no trivial development because, prior to the invention of these chronometers, clocks tended to rely on pendulums, and pendulums don't work on rocking and listing boats. Chronometers enabled sailors to take with them on their voyage the time at their point of origin. By comparing the time at the point of origin with the local time given by the position of the Sun, sailors could work out the time difference and therefore their longitude.

John Harrison, the autodidact who eventually won the longitude prize for his chronometers, faced a great many obstacles along the way, not least from rivals who favoured the astronomical approach (see Sobel, 2007 for an account of the longitude story). Nevertheless, he never dealt with the kinds of challenges that face advocates of systematic synthetic phonics and the reasons for this are instructive.

First, everyone could agree on the objective of determining longitude and how to test it. We don't have that with phonics. If a child cannot read, they don't crash into the rocks and die and this is a fundamental difference. It takes us time to notice. When mortality stalks us we tend to get real; relativists don't generally step in front of buses. With educational outcomes there is much more room to wiggle.

If a child doesn't learn to read then we may say they are not ready. We may perhaps suggest that they have a developmental disorder. This might indeed be true but how do we rule out the possibility that their failure to learn to read is due to the teacher pursuing a less effective teaching method?

Imagine John Harrison being informed that taking a chronometer on a voyage was boring and that dead reckoning was more fun; more engaging; more practical. After all, sailors *enjoy* throwing the ropes overboard; those unfortunate sailors who crash into rocks and die are suffering from a neurological disorder that means they mix up different aspects of dead reckoning. Imagine the claim that you can't really test the benefit of chronometers because sailors and ships are far too complicated and you need to take account of social relationships. Indeed, there is no such thing as a method for determining longitude because experienced sailors use, and have always used, a range of approaches. Perhaps we might give a number of chronometers to sailors, but even if we do, we can't be sure that they will all use them successfully. It is simply not predictable that a specific sailor will use a specific chronometer to correctly determine longitude because people are human and human beings are not deterministic in the way that atoms and pulleys are. Imagine a Harrison critic suggesting that Harrison was only advocating for the use of chronometers because he had chronometers to sell (while ignoring the sellers of knotted ropes). Imagine Harrison being accused of being an agent of the far-right who wanted to regulate time all across the globe in order to control people. Finally, imagine newspapers routinely presenting this as a debate between two sets of extremists, one as equally eccentric as the other and both removed from the reality of everyday life.

If you can imagine these things then you will have some idea of what it has been like to advocate for phonics teaching over the past century.

Digraphs and diphthongs

The contemporary practice of systematic synthetic phonics is highly advanced when compared with the phonics teaching that whole-word approaches sought to replace in the early 1900s. It is best considered a body of knowledge rather than a teaching method. What we perceive to be the 'skill' of lifting words off the page is actually the automatic retrieval and application of lots of elements of phonics knowledge. Systematic synthetic phonics programmes aim to make this knowledge explicit, teach it explicitly and practise it to mastery – the point when it can be retrieved and applied without effort.

When we make the knowledge of how language works explicit in this way, we need terms to describe it. In this chapter, I have already mentioned the concept of a 'grapheme' and a 'phoneme'. Phonics teachers regular discuss 'GPCs' or grapheme–phoneme correspondences. But this is not enough.

To accurately teach reading via a systematic synthetic phonics approach, and to be able to discuss this teaching with colleagues, teachers need to be aware of a whole range of terms. For instance, they need to know that a 'digraph' is a grapheme made up of two letters. They need to know that a diphthong is sound made-up of two vowel sounds, as well as how to recognise a diphthong in speech. They need to know about the 'schwa' vowel sound because this is linked to problems children have with spellings. They need to know what a 'morpheme' is – the smallest unit of meaning – and how this differs from a 'grapheme'. They need etymological knowledge such as the origin language of a word; is it Anglo-Saxon, French or perhaps Latin?

Teachers are unlikely to acquire this knowledge during their own time as a school student unless they happen to study a linguistics course, and so it would seem incumbent on universities to teach this content on teacher education courses for primary school teachers, as well as perhaps courses for all teachers of English.

We have a small amount of research that seeks to determine what it is that new teachers, as well as more experienced teachers, know of this area and this research is not encouraging. For instance, one study of a sample of teachers in the Australian state of Victoria found that most of them displayed limited phonics knowledge, despite generally rating their ability to teach phonics and related skills as moderate or good (Stark et al., 2016). A different study ambitiously sought to sample final year early childhood and primary education students from across Australian universities. Those who responded displayed minimal to very poor knowledge of early reading, a finding similar to that of comparable research (Meeks and Kemp, 2017).

If you are preparing to teach early reading and you are unfamiliar with the terms in this chapter then you are not alone. However, you have the advantage of knowing that you lack this knowledge and therefore the potential to do something about it.

Conclusion

Teaching reading is a fundamental act of schooling. Reading ability underpins all academic endeavour and so reading failure will largely cut a child adrift from an academic education. The objective of bringing literacy to the masses is an egalitarian, anti-elitist project worthy of all teachers with a social conscience and it was this objective that led to the advent of public education systems in the first place. It would therefore seem reasonable to suggest that if our schools are able to do nothing else, they should be capable of teaching reading effectively. This is not the case.

Ultimately, this situation is hard to fathom. It seems likely that we are simply the victims of a proliferation of bad ideas. When evidence is presented that demonstrates that these ideas are bad, it is easier, and far more human, to rationalise this away than it is to deal with the emotional burden of being wrong. It is hard to be that teacher who, with the very best of intentions, did not do the best for his or her students. We want to be the heroes of our own stories and not fools or villains. If we can understand this dynamic and appreciate that there is nothing inevitable about the situation we are in – that we could actually be far more effective at teaching reading – then we can see how this example applies to education more generally. We should set ego aside, read the research as it stands, call for better research where it is lacking and commit to heeding its findings, even if this means we were wrong.

References

Association of Masters of the Boston Public Schools, 1844. Remarks on the Seventh Annual Report of the Hon. Horace Mann, Secretary of the Massachusetts Board of Education.

Biemiller, A. (2003). Oral comprehension sets the ceiling on reading comprehension. *American Educator*, 27(1), 23.

Biesta, G.J., 2009. How to use pragmatism pragmatically? Suggestions for the twenty-first century. *Education and Culture*, 25(2), pp. 34–45.

Biesta, G.J., 2015. *The Beautiful Risk of Education*. Abingdon: Routledge.

Chall, J.S., 2000. *The Academic Achievement Challenge: What Really Works in the Classroom?* New York: Guilford Publications.

Cunningham, J.W., 2001. The national reading panel report. *Reading Research Quarterly*, 36(3), pp. 326–35.

Egan, K., 2004. *Getting It Wrong from the Beginning: Our Progressivist Inheritance from Herbert Spencer, John Dewey, and Jean Piaget*. New Haven, CT: Yale University Press.

Fox, M., 2008. *The Folly of Jolly Old Phonics*. [online] Available at: http://memfox.com/for-parents/for-parents-the-folly-of-jolly-old-phonics/.

Goodman, K. and Goodman, Y., 1976. Learning to read is natural. *Theory and Practice of Early Reading*, 1, pp. 137–54.

Hoover, W.A. and Gough, P.B., 1990. The simple view of reading. *Reading and Writing*, 2(2), pp. 127–60.

Johnston, F.R., 2000. Word learning in predictable text. *Journal of Educational Psychology*, 92(2), p. 248.

Kim, J. 2008 'Research and the reading wars', in F. Hess (ed.), *When Research Matters: How Scholarship Influences Education Policy*. Cambridge, MA: Harvard Education Press. pp. 89–111.

Krashen, S., 2002. Defending whole language: the limits of phonics instruction and the efficacy of whole language instruction. *Reading Improvement*, 39(1), pp. 32–42.

McGuinness, D., 2006. *Early Reading Instruction: What Science Really Tells Us about How to Teach Reading*. Cambridge, MA: MIT Press.

Meeks, L.J. and Kemp, C.R., 2017. How well prepared are Australian pre-service teachers to teach early reading skills? *Australian Journal of Teacher Education*, 42(11), p. 1. Available at: http://dx.doi.org/10.14221/ajte.2017v42n11.1.

Millard, A.R., 1986. The infancy of the alphabet. *World Archaeology*, 17(3), pp. 390–8.

National Reading Panel (US), National Institute of Child Health and Human Development (US), 2000. *Teaching Children to Read: An Evidence-Based Assessment of the Scientific Research Literature on Reading and Its Implications for Reading Instruction*. Bethesda, MD: National Institute of Child Health and Human Development, National Institutes of Health.

National Research Council, 1998. *Preventing Reading Difficulties in Young Children*. Washington, DC: National Academies Press.

Old, A., 2017. 3 ways phonics denialists will try to fool you. [online] Available at: https://teachingbattleground.wordpress.com/2017/11/25/3-ways-phonics-denialists-will-try-to-fool-you/.

Postgate, N., 1992. *Early Mesopotamia: Society and Economy at the Dawn of History*. Abingdon: Routledge.

Ravitch, D., 2001. *Left Back: A Century of Battles Over School Reform*. New York: Simon and Schuster.

Rose, J., 2006. *Independent Review of the Teaching of Early Reading: Final Report*. London: Department for Education and Skills.

Rosen, M., 2017. Dear Justine Greening, whatever happened to 'eradicating illiteracy'? *The Guardian*, 31 January. [online] Available at: www.theguardian.com/education/2017/jan/31/justine-greening-literacy-schools-phonics-teaching.

Rowe, K., 2005. *Teaching Reading: Report of the National Inquiry into the Teaching of Literacy (Australia)*. Australian Council for Educational Research. [online] Available at: https://research.acer.edu.au/tll_misc/5.

Sample, I. (2017). Oldest *Homo sapiens* bones ever found shake foundations of the human story. *The Guardian*, 7 June. [online] Available at: www.theguardian.com/science/2017/jun/07/oldest-homo-sapiens-bones-ever-found-shake-foundations-of-the-human-story.

Sobel, D., 2007. *Longitude: The True Story of a Lone Genius Who Solved the Greatest Scientific Problem of His Time.* New York: Bloomsbury Publishing USA.

Stark, H.L., Snow, P.C., Eadie, P.A. and Goldfeld, S.R., 2016. Language and reading instruction in early years' classrooms: the knowledge and self-rated ability of Australian teachers. *Annals of Dyslexia*, 66(1), pp. 28–54.

Tunmer, W.E. and Chapman, J.W., 2012. Does set for variability mediate the influence of vocabulary knowledge on the development of word recognition skills? *Scientific Studies of Reading*, 16(2), pp. 122–40.

Turner, M., Burkard, T. and Centre for Policy Studies, 1996. *Reading Fever: Why Phonics Must Come First.* London: Centre for Policy Studies.

Zimmer, B. (2010). Ghoti. *New York Times Magazine*, 25 June. [online] Available at: www.nytimes.com/2010/06/27/magazine/27FOB-onlanguage-t.html.

11

TO BE A TEACHER

Key Points

This chapter will:

- Examine why people go into teaching
- Discuss teacher workload
- Explore the emotional load that teaching imposes
- Suggest some ways of coping with these issues
- Ask whether teaching is a profession and discuss ways of making it more professional
- Assert that, despite the challenges, teaching is a highly rewarding occupation

Cows in the exam hall

We fall into teaching in different ways. I was never clear about what I wanted to do, right up until my final year of university. I applied for a teaching course because I thought that as a maths and science teacher, I would never be unemployed. But I didn't expect teaching would be my career.

This changed in Africa. I had been recruited by a group of students at my university to teach for a couple of months in Uganda in the summer of 1997. This was a bitter-sweet time. I soon realised that our group would do little lasting good. The schools lacked physics teachers, partly due to the AIDS epidemic, and so although we were needed, two months was just a drop in the ocean. Once we left, it was back to normal. Ultimately, the group leaders who recruited us admitted that the agenda was as much about converting us to their brand of evangelical Anglicanism as it was about helping Ugandans.

Teaching in Uganda was basic. We had textbooks to help plan the lessons, which I wrote out in an exercise book. I literally wrote down the things I intended to put on the board and the questions I intended to ask. That was all there was to it. I would go to class and make use of a blackboard with a wide crack transecting it, in order to communicate these ideas with words and diagrams. I even modulated my voice to make it easier to understand.

The final day, I set an exam. The exam hall was the school yard with desks arrayed in a grid pattern. The exam papers were produced with a spirit duplicator machine – I had to scratch the diagrams with a stylus. As the students answered my questions, a long-horned cow picked its way between the desks.

Although my religious views were unaffected by the experience, my view of teaching changed utterly. From being a fall-back option, teaching became my vocation. My first experiences in the classroom were joyful. The children were desperate to learn and for the first time, I had that feeling a teacher experiences when a child understands something they didn't understand before. That is the fulcrum on which all of teaching pivots and that's what set me on my path. I am sure my experiences in Uganda kept me going when I later developed my craft in less welcoming environments.

Although my particular experience may be unusual, it shares many of the themes that are present in research about why people choose to go in to teaching. Two broad categories emerge of intrinsic and altruistic motivations. Intrinsic motivations include a love of the subject you teach and a desire to continue to work in that area, and a love of working with children. Altruistic motivations include the idea of working to make society a better, perhaps more equitable, place. When asked, teachers tend to downplay the role of extrinsic motivators such as pay or holidays, but then perhaps they would do even if these factors are important to them, in order to preserve their own self-image and a positive image of the profession (Heinz, 2015).

I can recall meeting a late entrant into teaching in the staffroom of one of my previous schools – let's call him Julian. He was about to embark upon training through the Graduate Teacher Programme (GTP), a school-based route into teaching that used to be available in England and Wales. I asked him why he had decided to move from banking into teaching and he replied, without hesitation, that he wanted a better quality of life and better holidays. Needless to say, he didn't stay the course.

Martyrs

An empathy gap exists between teachers and non-teachers. At family gatherings in dining rooms across the English-speaking world there will be a teacher complaining about workload who will be put back in their box by a family member claiming that they should get out into the real world if they want to know what hard work *really* is, and anyway, what about the holidays?

Anecdotally, I know of a number of people like Julian who have switched into teaching from prestigious, highly paid careers and who find it a shock.

Compared to other professions, it may be that teaching is a particularly 'leaky' job in that it oozes out from the confines of the school day, into teachers' homes and onto their kitchen tables. Workload is certainly recognised as an issue by policymakers, with the UK government recently launching a consultation on how to reduce it (Reducing Teacher Workload, 2017).

The UK government identified three key areas that tend to inflate teacher workload: marking, planning and data management. From earlier chapters, it should be clear that current planning and marking practices are not efficient. However, for many people, these activities tend to define what it means to be a teacher and so attempts to reform them are met with defensiveness and guilt. Take away some of an English teacher's marking load and you take away part of their identity. We need to replace the martyr mindset that views teaching as being about carrying lots of exercise books around, with a mindset that focuses on something more fundamental: what our students learn.

Front-line teachers cannot solve workload on their own because these practices have usually become institutionalised across schools or school systems. For instance, until recently the English schools inspectorate heaped praise on schools operating unsustainable marking policies (Independent Teacher Workload Review Group, 2016). That has now changed under pressure from teachers. So there is hope for the future and we will return to this later.

Teaching is also hard emotional work. Rather than being about crossing some commonly accepted threshold of competence, teaching is more of a performance. Some teachers are better than others. Or perhaps I should claim that some teaching is better than other teaching. And yet this is extremely hard to measure. We know, for instance, that teachers who are associated with large learning gains in their students across one year do not necessarily see the same gains the next year (Berliner, 2014). We also know that attempts to evaluate teaching through observation are flawed, with even the most rigorous systems having only limited validity (Coe, 2014). Yet students, parents, other teachers, school leaders and inspectors form judgements about teaching all the time. Without a solid basis, these judgements can feel capricious, arbitrary and motivated by personal tastes and biases. Teachers need to learn not only to take these comments seriously, in a detached, professional way, but also to not take any one piece of feedback as definitive or dwell on it for too long. As a young teacher, I would tell myself 'I may not be as effective as I would like to be, but I am doing more good than if I quit teaching.' It was probably true and it helped adjust me to the numerous ups and downs.

Another source of the emotional load of teaching is in managing classroom behaviour and the behaviour of a minority of students who are deeply challenging on a personal level. Whatever the underlying cause of the behaviour, being told by a student that you are ineffective, boring, racist, sexist, sexually motivated, tastelessly dressed or physically flawed, or being sworn at, threatened, or having personal possessions stolen, are all issues that any teacher finds challenging, but that also hit particularly hard in the first few years before you have learned how to distance yourself from your role. It is worth bearing in mind that your students only see a small sliver of who you really are, so when you are on the receiving end of these kinds of comments, they are reacting to 'the teacher', using lines they have probably honed elsewhere. They are not really passing judgement on you as a person, no matter how personal it feels.

Concerns about behaviour regularly arise in surveys of classroom teachers and they are only usually eclipsed by concerns about workload (e.g. Rhodes et al., 2004). A comprehensive inquiry into government education provision in the Australian state of New South Wales took place in the early 2000s. It raised concerns about the bad behaviour of some students, stating that, 'The problem is serious, disrupts learning and drains the morale of staff. Many observers believe it is the single most important reason for parents transferring their children to private schools' (Vinson, 2002). One more recent survey of 41 new teachers in the Australian state of Victoria found that they 'did not … anticipate the degree of errant student behaviour, to the extent that many had to endure threats to their personal safety' (Latifoglu, 2014). Indeed, the Australian Teacher Education Ministerial Advisory Group (TEMAG), two Australian education thinktanks and a review of initial teacher education in England have all called for improved provision of training in classroom management for teachers (Craven et al., 2014; Carter, 2015; Goss et al., 2017; Joseph, 2017).

There are reasons to suspect the available evidence even underrepresents the impact of student behaviour on teachers. As we have seen, the dominant philosophical view in education derives, at least in part, from romanticism. In a reversal of the doctrine of original sin, romantics tended to see children as pure and innocent, corrupted only by adults. This plays out in a discourse around student behaviour that avoids holding students responsible for their actions. If a student misbehaves then this is a sign of trauma or it should be interpreted as a form of communication. Perhaps it is a signal that the adult in the room, the teacher, is not meeting the specific needs of that child. Perhaps the lesson is not engaging enough or appropriately differentiated. Such an atmosphere motivates teachers to lower expectations, turn a blind eye and keep quiet about behaviour problems, until and unless they become extreme in nature.

The other reason why the picture may be an underrepresentation is the increasing medicalisation of behaviour issues. The *Diagnostic and Statistical Manual of Mental Disorders* is a publication by the American Psychiatric Association that provides clinicians with a set of criteria by which to assess mental disorders. From its inception in 1952, through to the current version, DSM-5, the number of disorders listed has increased from 108 to 352 and the threshold for diagnosis has been lowered in many cases (Khoury et al., 2014).

Oppositional Defiant Disorder (ODD) is listed in DSM-5. It is diagnosed via 'A pattern of angry/irritable mood, argumentative/defiant behaviour, or vindictiveness lasting at least 6 months as evidenced by at least four symptoms'. The symptoms include being easily annoyed, angry, resentful and argumentative. Given that it is diagnosed through a pattern of behaviours, it cannot also explain those same behaviours because the logic of this would be circular. Instead, there would need to be some underlying cause. This could be one of many possibilities that may be unrelated. In a sense it is therefore a little like diagnosing someone with 'sneezing disorder' because they sneeze a lot – it doesn't tell you why the person is sneezing, something that could be caused by one of many allergies or by an infection.

There is a growing tendency to class mental disorders of this kind as a disability (e.g. Graham, 2016). Not only does this bring a lot more individuals under the scope of anti-discrimination laws or regulations, it can obscure meaning. For instance, when the Australian Education Union surveyed its members and claimed that 'Around 79% said training to teach students with a disability was only "of some help" or was "not helpful"', there is a chance that part of this finding relates to behaviour problems (Australian Education Union, 2017).

New teachers need to seek out a school that offers them support with behaviour issues. This does not necessarily mean a school without behaviour problems, but rather one that is clear and explicit about how behaviour is to be managed. No teacher will ever avoid the worry caused by students who behave in a disruptive and sometimes seemingly cruel way, but the support of senior colleagues makes a huge difference, as I found early in my own career. This should be an issue that a teacher asks about at interview and it should be something that bears heavily on whether to accept a job offer.

Is teaching a profession?

We commonly view occupations such as the law, engineering or medicine as 'professions'. Conversely, few would argue that being a car mechanic is a profession. So, what constitutes this difference and where does teaching sit?

First, we need to dismiss other meanings of 'professional'. Sometimes this is simply used to connote a good job done. At other times it draws a distinction between those who are paid and those who are amateurs, such as in sports. But these definitions cannot help us draw a distinction between a lawyer and a car mechanic.

Instead, it is often argued (e.g. Horsley and Thomas, 2003) that professionalism of the lawyerly kind rests upon the exercise of autonomy. States sanction a professional body, such as a Law Society, to regulate and set standards within the profession. Lawyers themselves are therefore in control of what it means to be a lawyer. This is autonomy at the level of the profession.

We can see that teaching is far from a profession in these terms. The bodies that regulate us and set our standards are usually arms of the state, peopled by non-teaching academics and bureaucrats.

However, autonomy may also be exercised at the individual level. A professional is generally considered to be someone who is trusted to make decisions and decide for themselves when to seek help and consult with others. In practical terms, teachers often exercise such individual autonomy. They can close the classroom door and get on with the job as they see fit. In fact, the education research literature is full of complaints about teachers who won't follow an agreed approach or adopt an innovation.

To an extent, this is healthy and wise. As we have seen, many innovations in education are ill-advised, based more upon philosophical notions of how education ought to be than upon scientific evidence of how learning occurs. Teachers who close the door and let the fads wash over them may, in many circumstances, be making the best choice for their students.

However, we should also be aware that the innovative practice of one generation of teachers may end up as the next generation's unquestioned common sense. You don't need to know the origin and evolution of an idea to subscribe to it. As the economist John Maynard Keynes put it, 'The ideas of economists and political philosophers, both when they are right and when they are wrong, are more power-ful than is commonly understood. Indeed the world is ruled by little else. Practical men, who believe themselves to be quite exempt from any intellectual influence, are usually the slaves of some defunct economist' (Keynes, 1936).

A good example of this phenomenon is reading instruction. A new, innovative whole-word approach to teaching reading can, over time, become the default, commonsense method. Teachers using such an approach and who resist a change to one based upon phonics, are not following the best path for their students. So, we cannot really say in the abstract that 'We should resist', or 'We should change'. Instead, teachers should be informed by the evidence. Teaching, if it is to fully become a profession, needs to develop mechanisms for more robustly evaluating the evidence behind its practices.

It is interesting to reflect upon the kinds of personal autonomy practised by lawyers or medical professionals. It should be immedi-ately clear that they cannot simply do whatever they like. Although they are invested with the power to make decisions, the regulatory function of the profession should strip them of their professional sta-tus if they started making bad ones. This is because these standards are well understood and explicit. Teaching standards, by contrast, tend to be vague.

Consider a surgeon about to perform a heart operation. She may have the authority to decide how to proceed but it is inconceivable that she would whimsically decide to do something a bit different or innovative. Most such operations follow a strict protocol, similar in many ways to the scripted lessons of Siegfried Engelmann. In his book *The Checklist Manifesto* Atul Gawande calls for a greater use of checklists in society at large, based on the experience of implement-ing them in medicine (Gawande, 2009). So, the idea that professions are characterised by high levels of individual autonomy may lead to a misunderstanding when applied to teaching.

Perhaps one of the reasons why there is a striking difference between the practices of education and those occupations that we unambiguously label as professions is that failure in education is slow to emerge. Badly engineered machines don't work or break down or hurt people. Bad medicine can cause people to die. Bad legal advice leads to legal action or lost court cases.

In contrast, what is the effect of relatively poor mathematics teach-ing on a group of eight-year-old students? Some will learn the maths anyway, either because they are able to pick it up implicitly or because they are helped at home. Those who do not learn in this environment may not be viewed as casualties of poor teaching, but rather as students with particular learning difficulties. Ultimately, the full effects of lower-quality teaching may not be discernible until adult life and the challenges that it provides. This may be why teachers are more able to exercise their individual autonomy to make poor choices.

Teaching is therefore in a liminal, twilight state, caught between an occupation and a profession. To fully become a profession, not only would teaching have to move towards regulating itself, it would also have to develop a shared understanding of which teaching actions are appropriate and which are not. This is not simply a case of making a list of ethical behaviours that teachers are expected to uphold, it would have to impinge upon the teaching of knowledge and skills in lessons. Teachers could then exercise individual autonomy within the strict professional parameters that this shared understanding provides. We are not there yet, caught as we are in a mix of grassroots eclecticism and top-down mandation.

A new movement for change

The only way to improve the professionalism of teaching is for teachers themselves to take control of the agenda. They are not in charge at present and we need to understand why this is the case if we are to move forward.

When asked, many teachers may express a lack of interest in education research. This is understandable given that their experiences with it have often led them to see it as impractical and abstruse. If it were impinging upon their everyday working lives then they may have more need to engage, but the closed-door, autonomous nature of many classrooms means that many teachers feel relatively unaffected.

Anecdotally, I am regularly contacted through my blog by teachers who are being subjected to a top-down reform that is claimed to be based on research evidence. Once teachers are asked to significantly change their practice, they become interested in the grounds for doing so. If more teachers knew the research evidence relevant to classroom management, marking, differentiation and different teaching strategies then I believe that they would find this interesting and important. The key is that the research must have practical implications.

An important change that has taken place during my career is the advent of social media. I am active on Twitter and there are groups of teachers who are active on Facebook. This has led to a flourishing movement based around blogs.

Social media has the power to cut through the atomised nature of teaching. Instead of receiving top-down pronouncements, a teacher in Idaho can talk directly to a teacher in Auckland about the best way to teach the particle theory of matter. There is nobody mediating this conversation; no gatekeepers controlling the flow of acceptable information.

Much of the teacher activity on social media could be described as 'Here's a Cool Activity'. There is nothing wrong with sharing resources and ideas with other teachers. It is often a necessary part of lesson planning, particularly for teachers in those schools where an irrational fear of textbooks predominates. There have been some strange and ethically fraught attempts to cash-in on this phenomenon, with teachers selling resources to other teachers. However, there is still a large, open-source community out there.

Perhaps more interestingly, there is a growing critical movement. Teachers have started to blog about research evidence and educational philosophy, often challenging established ideas in the process. Some of these teachers have then gone on to write books and speak at conferences.

A particularly intriguing development is the researchED movement. In 2013, a discussion on Twitter led to Tom Bennett, a UK teacher, setting up the first researchED conference. The conference was held on a Saturday so that teachers would be able to attend without taking time off school (and therefore without needing permission from their school leaders). Speakers, who included a mix of practising teachers and academics, spoke for free, keeping the ticket price down. Despite having to take time out of their weekend, over 500 people attended the first researchED conference. The movement has now grown. As well as the national conference, there are subject-specific conferences. And researchED has now visited a number of countries, including Canada, The Netherlands and Australia (researchED, 2018).

I have been involved with the Australian conferences and it is fair to say that the movement has not been universally and uncritically welcomed. In 2017, some comments in the promotional materials were highlighted by an academic on Twitter and others then joined in to express their outrage. The backlash failed, with the conference attracting its largest ever number of attendees to date, but it does suggest that some people are uncomfortable with teacher-led movements taking control of the education agenda (Ashman, 2017).

One of the systemic problems within education is that ambitious teachers who seek promotion will need to pursue roles that take them out of the classroom. This has been recognised as an issue for some time. High-status routes that keep teachers in the classroom have been introduced, including the UK's Advanced Skills Teacher status (Fuller et al., 2013), as well as Advanced Skills Teacher status in Australia and other initiatives across the globe. Unfortunately, these programmes suffer from the need to define skills and abilities that make one teacher better than another. Although there are plenty of subjective opinions about what these are, as we have seen, systematic attempts to measure them have proved disappointing.

A better approach may be to encourage more teachers to engage with education research. Teachers could be encouraged to study for master's and doctoral degrees that involve conducting original research. In ideal circumstances, these teachers would have a mandate within their schools to address questions of research. Their need to consider practical implementation issues would filter the kinds of research that they brought into their schools and avoid the more esoteric.

This could go badly wrong, with a new army of teacher-researchers busying themselves in conducting poorly designed research based more on philosophical principles than questions of effectiveness, particularly given the academic tastes of likely partner universities. So, I think it is too early to suggest this as a model for system reform. Instead, I would recommend that teachers pursue further research on an individual basis. I would recommend against the goal of doing a master's or doing a PhD and instead focus on the kinds of research that interest you. Then, seek out researchers who work in this field and see what your options might be. Imagine committing several years to a project that you grow deeply disillusioned with after a few months.

Nevertheless, the growing do-it-yourself, punk ethos among teachers that is being harnessed and facilitated by social media probably does represent the best chance we have of increasing our professionalism.

A matter of respect

Being a teacher is not the soft option – the easy life – that some people think it is. It can be physically and emotionally draining. For me, the most difficult period in the job was as a young teacher working in a challenging school in London. Poor behaviour was an issue and I did not always feel respected by the students.

One day, there was a rumour of a gang fight outside the school. Police arrived, some of them on mounted horses, and they tried to disperse the students in order to prevent trouble. I had never seen my students interact with the police before and I was shocked. 'You can't tell us where to stand!' was one of the more polite comments they snarled at the police as they generally tried to make the police officers' lives as difficult as possible. I approached a group of these students and, addressing them by their names, I asked them to do what the police asked. I explained that it was necessary because of the risk; that we had asked the police for help. 'OK, Sir,' they shrugged, sheepishly, and then moved along down the road.

Teachers might often feel as if they are not respected. But sometimes we are the adults who our students respect the most.

The rewards of teaching

It would a mistake to sound warnings about the most challenging parts of the job without mentioning the good bits.

One advantage of teaching is definitely the holidays. Of course, most teachers will spend a considerable amount of their holidays working but the point is that this is flexible time. If you want to work hard in the last couple of weeks of term, taking a few late nights, then you may be able to go and trek through Nepal for the whole of your break. The option is there because your time is flexible.

Interestingly, pay does not come up as a major factor in reviewing the research on teacher satisfaction. In my experience in the UK and Australia, pay is not extravagant, but it does seem commensurate with living a middle-class lifestyle, particularly outside of the areas with the highest house prices. I don't think anyone ever went into teaching to get rich and so the job just needs to pay enough that teachers are not worrying about how to make ends meet.

If you are interested in the subject or subjects you teach then that places you in a far better position than many people working in office jobs. When you add the unpredictable nature of children into the mix then this makes for a job that is rarely dull. Marking might be a chore at times, but I rarely hear teachers complaining that they had a boring day. If anything, teaching errs on the side of over- rather than under-stimulation.

In the right schools, there is a sense of camaraderie and purpose. Teachers offer support and advice to each other and help each other through the rough spells. Some schools also have a lively social scene that helps relieve the tensions of a tough week.

Teaching has a wider purpose. As a teacher, you contribute to the future of your community and to the nation. As you age, you start to bump into former students at the supermarket who often want to remember themselves to you and ask about how the old school is going. Teaching is one career in which you really do have a chance to change the world for the better.

And it all hinges on that fulcrum. For me, this is still the best part; seeing the lights go on when a student understands something important for the first time. I have done my job then. I have achieved time travel and stewarded important cultural knowledge from the past and into the future. It doesn't get any better than that.

Conclusion

Nobody should enter teaching under the illusion that it will be an easy job with long holidays. Teaching is intensely challenging. Some practices have grown up around teaching that, while not being particularly effective, demand a great deal of teachers' time. But it is not only workload that is an issue. Teaching can be emotionally demanding and some of the feedback that teachers will receive can feel intensely personal. A key strategy for dealing with this is to attempt to distance your personal and professional roles, so that criticism of your professional role can be dealt with more objectively.

Teaching is not quite a profession because it is not run by teachers. Although often quite autonomous at the individual level, teachers are subjected to top-down initiatives that would not be as great a feature of established professions, such as the law or medicine. Nevertheless, social media has now provided teachers with the opportunity to talk directly with each other and to start to take control of the agenda.

Teaching is deeply rewarding. It is rarely boring and it represents an opportunity to change the world for the better.

References

Ashman, G., 2017. ResearchED Melbourne 2017 sparks witch hunt. [Blog] *Filling the Pail*. Available at: https://gregashman.wordpress.com/2017/04/22/researched-melbourne-2017-sparks-witch-hunt/.

Australian Education Union, 2017. AEU demands greater investment in school leadership and teaching. Australian Education Union. [online] Available at: https://aeuvic.asn.au/aeu-demands-greater-investment-school-leadership-and-teaching.

Berliner, D.C., 2014. Exogenous variables and value-added assessments: a fatal flaw. *Teachers College Record*, 116(1), p. n1.

Carter, A., 2015. *Carter Review of Initial Teacher Training (ITT)*. DFE-00036-2015. London: Department for Education. Available at: www.gov.uk/government/uploads/system/uploads/attachment_data/file/399957/Carter_Review.pdf.

Coe, R., 2014. Classroom observation: it's harder than you think. Centre for Evaluation & Monitoring, CEMBlog, 9 January. Available at: www.cem.org/blog/414/.

Craven, G., Beswick, K., Fleming, J., Fletcher, T., Green, M., Jensen, B., Leinonen, E. and Rickards, F., 2014. *Action Now: Classroom Ready Teachers*. Teacher Education Ministerial Advisory Group. Australian Government, Department of Education and Training.

Fuller, C., Goodwyn, A. and Francis-Brophy, E., 2013. Advanced skills teachers: professional identity and status. *Teachers and Teaching*, 19(4), pp. 463–74.

Gawande, A., 2009. *The Checklist Manifesto*. New York: Metropolitan Books.

Goss, P., Sonnemann, J. and Griffiths, K., 2017. *Engaging Students: Creating Classrooms that Improve Learning*. Melbourne, VA: Grattan Institute.

Graham, L., 2016. Children with disabilities risk being misdiagnosed in order to receive school funding support. The Conversation. [online] Available at: https://theconversation.com/children-with-disabilities-risk-being-misdiagnosed-in-order-to-receive-school-funding-support-53490.

Heinz, M., 2015. Why choose teaching? An international review of empirical studies exploring student teachers' career motivations and levels of commitment to teaching. *Educational Research and Evaluation*, 21(3), pp. 258–97.

Horsley, M. and Thomas, D., 2003. Professional regulation and professional autonomy: benchmarks from across the professions – the New South Wales experience. *Change: Transformations in Education*, 6(1), pp. 34–47.

Independent Teacher Workload Review Group, 2016. Eliminating unnecessary workload around marking. [online] Department for Education. Available at: www.gov.uk/government/uploads/system/uploads/attach ment_data/file/511256/Eliminating-unnecessary-workload-around-marking.pdf.

Joseph, B., 2017. Research Report Snapshot: Getting the most out of Gonski 2.0: the evidence base for school investments. The Centre for Independent Studies, Sydney, NSW. Available at: www.cis.org.au/app/uploads/2017/10/rr31-snapshot-e.pdf?.

Keynes, J., 1936. *The General Theory of Employment, Interest and Money*. London: Macmillan.

Khoury, B., Langer, E.J. and Pagnini, F. (2014). The DSM: mindful science or mindless power? A critical review. *Frontiers in Psychology*, 5, p. 602.

Latifoglu, A., 2014. Staying or leaving? An analysis of early career paths of beginning teachers in victorian government secondary schools. Doctoral dissertation. University of Melbourne, Melbourne Graduate School of Education.

Reducing Teacher Workload, 2017. [online] Department for Education. Available at: www.gov.uk/government/publications/reducing-teachers-workload/reducing-teachers-workload.

ResearchED, 2018. Our story. [online] https://researched.org.uk/about/our-story/.

Rhodes, C., Nevill, A. and Allan, J., 2004. Valuing and supporting teachers: a survey of teacher satisfaction, dissatisfaction, morale and retention in an English local education authority. *Research in Education*, 71(1), pp. 67–80.

Vinson, T., 2002. *Inquiry into the Provision of Public Education in NSW: Report of the 'Vinson Inquiry'*. Sydney: Pluto Press Australia in conjunction with NSW Teachers Federation.

INDEX